951
T48

The Book and the Author

Atrocity stories are the vicious commonplace of war propaganda. The author and compiler of this book is well aware of that fact. *Japanese Terror in China* is *not* an atrocity tale. It is a collection of materials, intended for the *Manchester Guardian*, which the Japanese censors refused to pass. And with good reason—for these are authentic, documented accounts of neutral eyewitnesses (missionaries, businessmen, etc.) to Japan's occupation of North China. Mr. Timperley has one undying purpose—to have the civilian population of the world know, in all its details, exactly what a modern war of aggression is like. There is no rhetorical denunciation here—merely the sickening factual record from day to day and hour to hour.

Mr. Timperley is an Australian citizen. He has been in China, Manchuria, and Japan almost continuously since 1921. China correspondent for the *Manchester Guardian*, he is also an advisory editor of *Asia* magazine, and a contributor to *Foreign Affairs* and *Pacific Affairs*.

From the British Reviews:

"Certain to make a tremendous impression. . . . A documentary record of the most terrible atrocities that have ever stained the long and evil record of war."
—Edinburgh *Evening News*.

"The evidence . . . here put forward is quite clearly genuine and reliable."
—London *Times*.

"Surely there is no man so toughly insensitive as to be capable of reading straight through this appalling compilation of horrors. . . . What is happening in the Far East is, as Mr. Timperley points out, not a distant, academic horror; it is something which concerns us all."
—*Oxford Mail*.

"Its veracity cannot be questioned."
—*Manchester Guardian*.

"A reputable journalist like Mr. Timperley does not send out such messages without making sure of his facts. . . . The reports are bald statements of fact, and if anything probably underestimate the case. . . ."
—*Times Literary Supplement*.

JAPANESE TERROR IN CHINA

JAPANESE TERROR IN CHINA

Compiled and Edited by
H. J. TIMPERLEY
China Correspondent, *Manchester Guardian*

MODERN AGE BOOKS, INC.
NEW YORK

"Those who thus appreciate true valor should in their daily intercourse set gentleness first and aim to win the love and esteem of others. If you affect valor and act with violence, the world will in the end detest you and look upon you as wild beasts. Of this you should take heed."—Extract from Para. 3 of *The Imperial Precept to the Soldiers and Sailors,* issued by the Emperor Meiji on January 4, 1883. Authorized English translation on page 228 of *The Japan Year Book,* 1937. (This is read over to all units of the Japanese Army at frequent intervals in peacetime.)

FOREWORD

PERHAPS THIS BOOK would not have come to be written had it not been for the fact that telegrams reporting the outrages committed against Chinese civilians by the Japanese troops which occupied Nanking in December of last year were suppressed by the censors installed by the Japanese authorities in the foreign cable offices at Shanghai. Among the messages that were thus suppressed or mutilated were several telegrams which the writer attempted to send to the *Manchester Guardian*.

Although I was fully satisfied that the information upon which my messages were based was irrefutable, as the Japanese authorities had alleged some of them to be "grossly exaggerated," I began to search for documentary proof and had no difficulty in discovering a wealth of corroborative evidence from unimpeachable sources. So shocking was the state of affairs thus revealed that I conceived the notion of publishing this evidence forthwith.

I make this personal explanation in order to show that the idea of producing this book was entirely my own and, while I have received valuable assistance from several friends in the selection and compilation of the material, I take full responsibility for its publication. Access to the International Committee's correspondence was made possible through my connection with certain relief organizations in Shanghai which had received copies in order that they might understand the situation and cooperate as effectively as possible with the Nanking group. It was only at my earnest request that the custodians of these documents permitted me to make use of the material in this way.

It is by no means the purpose of this book to stir up animosity against the Japanese people. I have many Japanese friends whom I hold in the highest respect and I wish it were politic to mention their names. One in particular is an important official and another of rare fineness of intellect and feeling holds a semiofficial position in Shanghai. It was my privilege to be associated with them both in more than one humanitarian enterprise and I wish to express my heartfelt appreciation of their sympathetic cooperation and friendship under very trying circumstances. I should like also to pay a special tribute to a certain Japanese Army officer who, in private, expressed his regret at the massacre of the unfortunate Chinese civilians who were bombed in a refugee train near Sungkiang in the early part of last September. These men, and there must be many others like them, are doubly deserving of admiration and respect since to betray their true thoughts and feelings to their countrymen at a time like this may well bring them death and dishonor.

The aim of this book is to give the world as accurately as possible the facts about the Japanese Army's treatment of the Chinese civilian population in the 1937-8 hostilities so that war may be recognized for the detestable business it really is and thus be stripped of the false glamour with which militarist megalomaniacs seek to invest it.

Revelations of the propaganda methods used by both sides in other wars have not unnaturally caused many people to regard with scepticism any "atrocity" stories. In this volume are gathered statements, reports and documents, the most pertinent of which have been supplied by absolutely reliable neutral observers. The private letters have been left largely as they were written except where references were made to matters primarily of a personal nature and of concern only to the relatives and friends to whom the letters were addressed. As a matter of expediency and for the safety of all concerned, internal evidence of the identity of most of the writers has been suppressed. The official documents in Appendix D, however, are given in full. The originals or certified copies of these letters and documents have been examined by me and are being held in safekeeping. Photographs, motion picture films and other supporting evidence are also on record.

It remains only to express my personal thanks to those whose counsel or assistance I have sought in connection with the preparation of this volume, which is dedicated to the cause of collective security and to the prevention, through that means, of horrors such as it has been a painful task to set forth in these pages.

H. J. TIMPERLEY

Shanghai,
    March 23, 1938.

CONTENTS

CHAPTER

      Foreword 9

   I   Nanking's Ordeal 15

  II   Robbery, Murder and Rape 33

 III   Promise and Performance 46

 IV   The Nightmare Continues 52

   V   Terror in North China 61

 VI   Cities of Dread 71

 VII   Death From the Air 98

VIII   Organized Destruction 118

      Conclusion 134

APPENDIX

  A   Case Reports Covering Chapters II and III . . . 143

  B   Case Reports Covering Chapter V 157

  C   Case Reports Covering Period January 14, 1938, to February 9, 1938 161

  D   Correspondence Between Safety Zone Committee and Japanese Authorities, etc. 167

  E   The Nanking "Murder Race" 216

  F   How the Japanese Reported Conditions in Nanking . 218

CHAPTER I

NANKING'S ORDEAL

As a consequence of the Sino-Japanese hostilities which began in the summer of 1937, some eighteen million people were forced to flee from their homes in and around Shanghai, Soochow and Wusih, in August, September, October, and during the course of November and December from Hangchow, Chinkiang, Wuhu and Nanking. Camps were established by Chinese and foreigners in the Shanghai International Settlement and French Concession which fed and housed, at their height, some 450,000 destitute Chinese refugees.

At least 300,000 Chinese military casualties for the Central China campaign alone and a like number of civilian casualties were suffered. The countryside was depopulated and barren and the Japanese marched on hoping to catch up with wealth or with a disintegrating Chinese army to destroy. They found neither. The Chinese army withdrew and was reorganized within the next few months. The wealth of China, being largely the industrious character of her people whom the Japanese were chasing further into the interior with every step of their advance, and the factories they so carefully bombed and shelled to pieces, escaped them too.

In all this tale of misery there was one hope of peace and security for a small proportion of the bewildered peasants and townsmen and that was to reach a foreign supervised safety zone of some sort. Father Jacquinot de Besange had succeeded in establishing one such zone in November for 250,000 inhabitants of the devastated areas in the southern quarter of Shanghai.

During November, 1937, a small group of public-spirited residents of Nanking met and discussed the possibility of establishing a similar zone in Nanking where Chinese and foreigners could take refuge. The idea had already been debated as regards safety from aerial

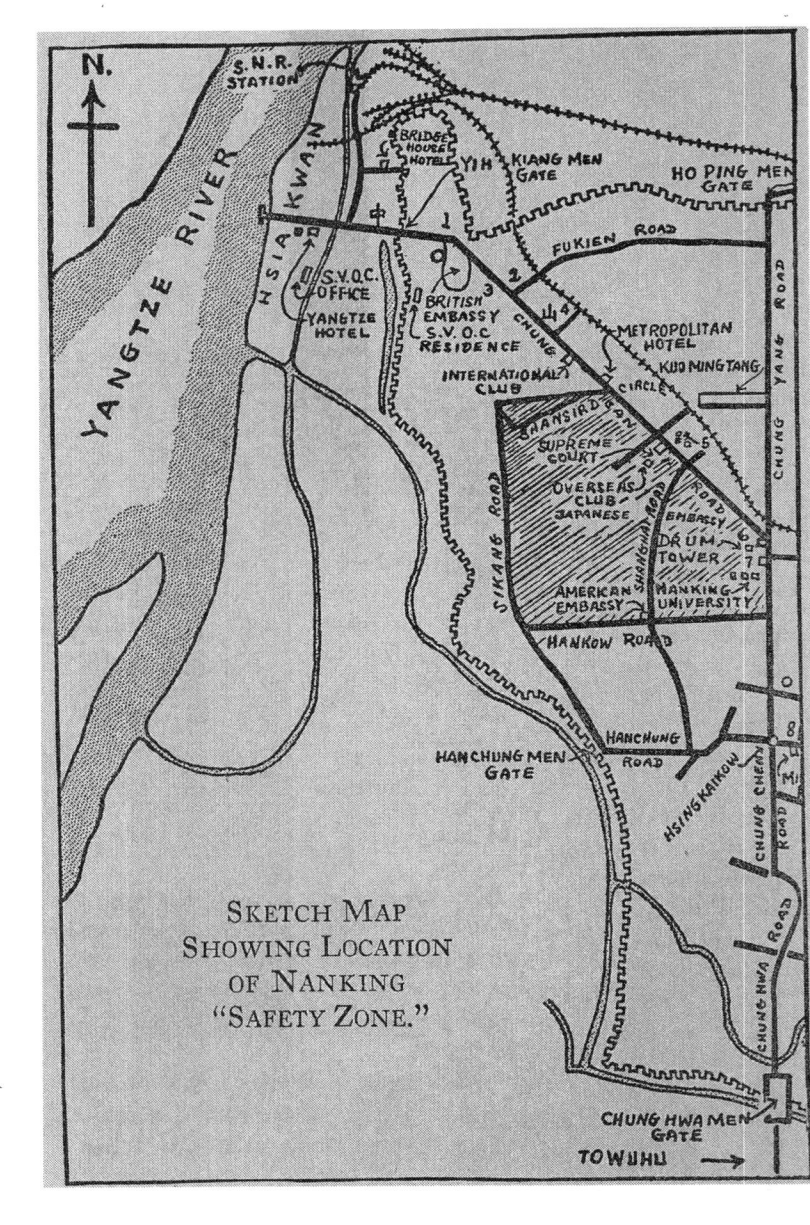

Sketch Map Showing Location of Nanking "Safety Zone."

bombing. No useful conclusions had been reached but with the approach of the Japanese troops the urgency of the problem was such that a committee was formed to establish this zone in the hope that, thereafter, it would be possible to obtain its recognition by both Chinese and Japanese.

From this seed grew the International Committee for the Nanking Safety Zone, whose Chairman was Mr. John H. D. Rabe, a German business man, and the names of whose other members are given in the list on page 169. Working in close conjunction with this Committee was the International Red Cross Committee of Nanking the names of whose members are also given in a list hereafter. (See page 170.)

To these veritable heroes, numbering just over a score, praise is due at the outset. How well it is deserved will be seen as their story is told. They elected, against the advice of their officials, to stay behind in Nanking, whence all, Chinese and foreign, who could find any means of transport, were fleeing in their hundreds of thousands. While none of them could have foreseen the actual events that occurred, all were men and women of experience and knowledge and could but know the danger of their position. Their courage, their selflessness, their devotion, and above all their determination to save something from the catastrophe that they knew conquest and subjection must mean for Nanking, will be apparent to all who read this account.

The area of the Safety Zone and its location are shown in the map on page 16. In Appendix D will be found copies of the letters which were written by the Zone Committee to Japanese officials on a variety of subjects together with a small selection of letters to other officials and institutions. No replies were ever received in

---

The sketch map opposite, reproduced in part by special permission from the *Shanghai Evening Post and Mercury,* shows the location of the "Safety Zone" established in Nanking by the International Committee. The zone measured three kilometers from North to South and two from East to West. Its total area was 3.86 square kilometers. The boundaries were all well-marked roads excepting the South-west corner, which was an imaginary line over the hills. Inside these limits were the compounds of the Japanese, American and Italian Embassies, the Netherlands Legation, the Ministry of Justice, the Supreme Court, the University of Nanking with its hospital, Ginling College and a number of other foreign mission institutions.

writing to these communications and only evasive verbal acknowledgment was ever made.

On December 13, exactly one month after it had smashed the Chinese defense of Shanghai, the Japanese army entered the gates of Nanking, the Chinese capital, some two hundred miles distant. This notable feat might well have gone down into history as one of the most spectacular military achievements of modern times. Actually whatever credit might have been due on this score was gravely discounted by the outrageous conduct of the Japanese troops in the cities which they occupied. As the Japanese army approached Nanking their airplanes distributed pamphlets declaring that "the Japanese troops exert themselves to the utmost to protect good citizens and to enable them to live in peace, enjoying their occupations." On December 10, in calling upon General Tang Seng-chih to surrender the city, General Iwane Matsui, Commander of the attacking forces, had declared: "Though harsh and relentless to those who resist, the Japanese troops are kind and generous to noncombatants and to Chinese troops who entertain no enmity to Japan." To what extent the Japanese army lived up to these glib assurances the following account will reveal. This brief but illuminating description of events immediately after the Japanese entry of Nanking is taken from a letter dated December 15, written to friends in Shanghai by one of the most respected members of Nanking's foreign community who is noted for his fairmindedness:

At Nanking the Japanese Army has lost much of its reputation, and has thrown away a remarkable opportunity to gain the respect of the Chinese inhabitants and of foreign opinion. The disgraceful collapse of Chinese authority and the break-up of the Chinese armies in this region left vast numbers of persons ready to respond to the order and organization of which Japan boasts. Many local people freely expressed their relief when the entry of Japanese troops apparently brought an end to the strains of war conditions and the immediate perils of bombardment. At least they were rid of their fears of disorderly Chinese troops, who indeed passed out without doing severe damage to most parts of the city.

But in two days the whole outlook has been ruined by frequent murder, wholesale and semiregular looting, and uncontrolled disturbance of private homes including offences against the security of women. Foreigners who have travelled over the city report many civilian bodies lying in the streets. In the central portion of Nanking they were counted yesterday as about one to the city block. A considerable percentage of the dead civilians were the victims of shooting or bayoneting in the afternoon and evening of the 13th, which was the time of the Japanese entry into the city. Any persons who ran in fear or excitement, and any one who was caught in streets or alleys after dusk by roving patrols was likely to be killed on the spot. Most of this severity was beyond even theoretical excuse. It proceeded in the Safety Zone as well as elsewhere, and many cases are plainly witnessed by foreigners and by reputable Chinese. Some bayonet wounds were barbarously cruel.

Squads of men picked out by Japanese troops as former Chinese soldiers have been tied together and shot. These soldiers had discarded their arms, and in some cases their military clothing. Thus far we have found no trace of prisoners in Japanese hands other than such squads, actually or apparently on the way to execution, save for men picked up anywhere to serve as temporary carriers of loot and equipment. From one building in the refugee zone, four hundred men were selected by the local police under compulsion from Japanese soldiers, and were marched off tied in batches of fifty between lines of riflemen and machine gunners. The explanation given to observers left no doubt as to their fate.

On the main streets the petty looting of the Chinese soldiers mostly of food shops and of unprotected windows, was turned into systematic destruction of shop-front after shop-front under the eyes of Japanese officers. Japanese soldiers needed private carriers to help them struggle along under great loads. Food was apparently in first demand, but everything else useful or valuable had its turn. Thousands upon thousands of private houses all through the city, occupied and unoccupied, large and small, Chinese and foreign, have been impartially plundered. Peculiarly disgraceful cases of robbery by soldiers include the following: scores of refugees in camps and shelters had money and valuables removed from their slight possessions during mass searches; the staff of the University Hospital were stripped of cash and watches from their persons, and of other possessions from the nurses' dormitory (their buildings are American, and like a number of others that were plundered, were flying foreign flags and carrying official proclamations from their respective Embassies); the seizure of motorcars and other property after tearing down the flags upon them.

There are reported many cases of rape and insult to women, which we have not yet had time to investigate. But cases like the following are sufficient to show the situation. From a house close to one of our foreign friends, four girls were yesterday abducted by soldiers. Foreigners saw in the quarters of a newly arrived officer, in a part of the city practically deserted by ordinary people, eight young women.

Under these conditions the terror is indescribable, and lectures by suave officers on their "sole purpose of making war on the oppressive Chinese Government for the sake of the Chinese people," leave an impression that nauseates.

Surely this horrible exhibition in Nanking does not represent the best achievement of the Japanese Empire, and there must be responsible Japanese statesmen, military and civilians, who for their own national interests will promptly and adequately remedy the harm that these days have done to Japanese standing in China. There are individual soldiers and officers who conduct themselves as gentlemen worthy of their profession and worthy of their Empire. But the total action has been a sad blow.

Further details are given in the following vivid account by a foreign resident of Nanking who has spent almost the whole of his life in China. His letter has been left exactly as it was received by his friends in Shanghai except that references of a largely personal nature have been deleted.

Nanking, China.
Xmas Eve, 1937.

What I am about to relate is anything but a pleasant story: in fact it is so very unpleasant that I cannot recommend anyone without a strong stomach to read it. For it is a story of such crime and horror as to be almost unbelievable, the story of the depredations of a horde who have been, and now are, working their will, unrestrained, on a peaceful, kindly, law-abiding people. Yet it is a story which I feel must be told, even if it is seen by only a few. I cannot rest until I have told it, and, perhaps fortunately, I am one of a very few who are in a position to tell it. It is not complete—only a small part of the whole; and God alone knows when it will be finished. I pray it may be soon—but I am afraid it is going to go on for many months to come, not just here but in other parts of China. I believe it has no parallel in modern history.

It is now Xmas Eve. I shall start with say December 10th. In these two short weeks we here in Nanking have been through a siege; the Chinese army has left, defeated, and the Japanese has come in. On that day Nanking was still the beautiful city we were so proud of, with law and order still prevailing: today it is a city laid waste, ravaged, completely looted, much of it burned. Complete anarchy has reigned for ten days—it has been a hell on earth. Not that my life has been in serious danger at any time; though turning lust-mad, sometimes drunken, soldiers out of houses where they were raping the women, is not altogether a safe occupation; nor does one feel, perhaps, too sure of himself when he finds a bayonet at his chest or a revolver at his head and knows it is handled by someone who heartily wishes him out of the way. For the Japanese Army is anything but pleased at our being here after having advised all foreigners to get out. They wanted no observers. But to have to stand by while even the very poor are having their last possession taken from them—their last coin, their last bit of bedding (and it is freezing weather), the poor ricksha man his ricksha; while thousands of disarmed soldiers who had sought sanctuary with you together with many hundreds of innocent civilians are taken out before your eyes to be shot or used for bayonet practice and you have to listen to the sound of the guns that are killing them; while a thousand women kneel before you crying hysterically, begging you to save them from the beasts who are preying on them; to stand by and do nothing while your flag is taken down and insulted, not once but a dozen times, and your own home is being looted; and then to watch the city you have come to love and the institution to which you had planned to devote your best deliberately and systematically burned by fire,—this is a hell I had never before envisaged.

We keep asking ourselves "How long can this last?" Day by day we are assured by the officials that things will be better *soon*, that "we will do our best"—but each day has been worse than the day before. And now we are told that a new division of 20,000 men is arriving. Will they have to have their toll of flesh and loot, of murder and rape? There will be little left to rob, for the city has been well-nigh stripped clean. For the past week the soldiers have been busy loading their trucks with what they wanted from the stores and then setting fire to the buildings. And then there is the harrowing realization that we have only enough rice and flour for the 200,000 refugees for another three weeks and coal for ten days. Do you wonder that one awakes in the night in a cold sweat of fear and sleep for the rest of the night is gone? Even if we had food enough for three months, how are they going to be fed after that? And with their homes burned, where are they going to live? They cannot continue much longer in their present terribly crowded condition; disease and pestilence must soon follow if they do.

Every day we call at the Japanese Embassy and present our protests, our appeals, our lists of authenticated reports of violence and crime. We are met with suave Japanese courtesy, but actually the officials there are powerless. The victorious army must have its rewards—and those rewards are to plunder, murder, rape, at will, to commit acts of unbelievable brutality and savagery on the very people they have come to protect and befriend, as they have so loudly proclaimed to the world. In all modern history surely there is no page that will stand so black as that of the rape of Nanking.

To tell the whole story of these past ten days would take too long. The tragic thing is that by the time the truth gets out to the rest of the world it will be cold—it will no longer be "news." Anyway, the Japanese have undoubtedly been proclaiming abroad that they have established law and order in a city that had already been looted and burned, and that the downtrodden population had received their benevolent army with open arms and a great flag-waving welcome. However, I am going to record some of the more important events of this period as I have jotted them down in my little diary, for they will at least be of interest to some of my friends and I shall have the satisfaction of having a permanent record of these unhappy days. It will probably extend beyond the date of this letter, for I do not anticipate being able to get this off for some considerable time. The Japanese censorship will see to that! Our own Embassy officials and those of other countries together with some of the business men who went aboard the ill-fated "Panay"[1] and the Standard Oil boats and other ships just before the capture of Nanking, confidently expecting to return within a week when they left, are still cooling their heels (those who haven't been killed or wounded by Japanese bombs and machine guns) out on the river or perhaps in one of the ports. We think it will be another fortnight before any of them is permitted to return, and longer than that before any of us is permitted to leave Nanking. We are virtually prisoners here.

You will recall, those of you who have read earlier letters of mine, that our International Committee for Nanking Safety Zone had been negotiating with both the Chinese and Japanese for the recognition of a certain area in the city which would be kept free of soldiers and all military offices and which would not be bombed or shelled, a place where the remaining two hundred thousand of Nanking's population of one million could take refuge when things became too hot, for it had become quite obvious that the splendid resistance which the Chinese had put up for so long at Shanghai was now broken and their morale largely gone. The terrific punishment which they had taken from the superior artillery, tanks and air forces could not be endured forever and the successful landing of Japanese troops on Hankchow Bay, attacking their flank and rear, was the crowning event in their undoing. It seemed inevitable that Nanking must soon fall.

On December 1 Mayor Ma[2] virtually turned over to us the administrative responsibilities for the Zone together with a police force of 450 men, 30,000 piculs (2,000 tons) of rice, 10,000 bags

[1] The American River Gunboat U.S.S. "Panay" was bombed and sunk by Japanese airplanes near Hohsien, about twenty-five miles up the Yangtze River from Nanking, on December 12, 1937.

[2] Ma Tsao-tsing.

of flour, and some salt, also a promise of £100,000 in cash, £80,000 of which was subsequently received. Gen. Tang,[1] recently executed we have been told, charged with the defence of the city, cooperated splendidly on the whole in the very difficult task of clearing the Zone of the military and anti-aircraft, and a most commendable degree of order was preserved right up to the very last moment when the Japanese began, on Sunday the 12th, to enter the walls. There was no looting save in a small way by soldiers who were in need of provisions, and foreign property throughout the city was respected. We had city water until the 10th, electricity until the following day, and telephone service actually up to the date the Japanese entered the city. At no time did we feel any serious sense of danger, for the Japanese seemed to be avoiding the Zone with their air bombs and shells, and Nanking was a heaven of order and safety as compared with the hell it has been ever since the Japanese came. It is true we had some difficulty with our trucking —the rice was stored outside the city and some of our drivers did not relish going out where the shells were falling. One lost an eye with a splinter of shrapnel, and two of our trucks were seized by the military, but that was a nothing compared with the difficulties we have since faced.

On December 10, the refugees were streaming into the Zone. We had already filled most of the institutional buildings—Ginling College, the War College and other schools, and now had to requisition the Supreme Court, the Law College and the Overseas buildings, forcing doors where they were locked and appointing our own caretakers. Two Japanese blimps were visible just beyond Purple Mountain, probably to direct artillery fire. Heavy guns were pounding the south gate, and shells were dropping into the city. Several shells landed just within the Zone to the south the following morning, killing about forty near the Bible Teachers' Training School and the Foo Chong Hotel. Mr. Sperling,[2] our Inspector, a German, was slightly injured at the latter place where

[1] General Tang Seng-chih. The report of his execution proved to be unfounded.
[2] Eduard Sperling, German, representative of Shanghai Insurance Co.

he was living. The U.S.S. "Panay" moved upriver, but before it left I had a phone call (the last city gate had been closed and we had forfeited our right to go aboard the gunboat) from Paxton[1] of our Embassy, giving me the last two navy radiograms to reach Nanking. He was phoning from outside the city, of course. The messages were from Wilbur and Boynton.

We were now a community of twenty-seven—eighteen Americans, five Germans, one Englishman, one Austrian and two Russians. Out on the river was the "Panay" with the two remaining Embassy men, Atcheson[2] and Paxton, and half a dozen others; the Standard Oil and Asiatic Petroleum motor-ships with many more, a hulk which had been fitted out as sort of a floating hotel and towed upstream with some twenty foreigners including Dr. Rosen[3] of the German Embassy and some four hundred Chinese, and other craft. All were looking forward to an early return to the city. How many of them have met their fate we do not know, but it will be a long time before any of them get back now. And what a Nanking they will see!

On Sunday the 12th I was busy at my desk in the Safety Zone all day long. We were using the former residence of Gen. Chang Chun, recently Minister of Foreign Affairs, as headquarters, so were very comfortably fixed, and incidentally had one of the best bombproof dugouts in all Nanking.

Airplanes had been over us almost constantly for the past two days, but no one heeded them now, and the shell fire had been terrific. The wall had been breached and the damage in the southern part of the city was tremendous. No one will ever know what the Chinese casualties were but they must have been enormous. The Japanese say they themselves lost forty thousand men taking Nanking. The general rout must have started early that afternoon. Soldiers streamed through the city from the south, many of them passing through the Zone, but they were well behaved and orderly. Gen. Tang asked our assistance in arranging a truce with the Japanese

[1] J. Hall Paxton, Second Secretary of the American Embassy.
[2] George Atcheson, Jr., Second Secretary of the American Embassy, temporarily in charge of the Embassy.
[3] Dr. George Rosen, German Embassy.

and Mr. Sperling agreed to take a flag and message—but it was already too late. He (Tang) fled that evening, and as soon as the news got out disorganization became general. There was panic as they made for the gate to Hsiakwan and the river. The road for miles was strewn with the equipment they cast away—rifles, ammunition, belts, uniforms, cars, trucks,—everything in the way of army impediments. Trucks and cars jammed, were overturned, caught fire; at the gate more cars jammed and were burned—a terrible holocaust,—and the dead lay feet deep. The gate blocked, terror-mad soldiers scaled the wall and let themselves down on the other side with ropes, puttees and belts tied together, clothing torn to strips. Many fell and were killed. But at the river was perhaps the most appalling scene of all. A fleet of junks was there. It was totally inadequate for the horde that was now in a frenzy to cross to the north side. The overcrowded junks capsized, then sank; thousands drowned. Other thousands tried to make rafts of the lumber on the river front, only to suffer the same fate. Other thousands must have succeeded in getting away, but many of these were probably bombed by Japanese planes a day or two later.

One small detail of three companies rallied under their officers, crossed the San Chia Ho, three miles up river, and tried to attack the Japanese forces that were coming in from that direction, but were outnumbered and practically decimated. Only one seems to have succeeded in getting back. He happened to be the brother of a friend of mine and appeared in my office the next morning to report the story. A fellow officer had drowned while the two of them were trying to swim the small tributary to the Yangtze which they had crossed before on rafts. And before daylight he had managed to scale the wall and slip in unobserved.

So ended the happy, peaceful, well ordered, progressive regime which we had been enjoying here in Nanking and on which we had built our hopes for still better days. For the Japanese were already in the city and with them came terror and destruction and death. They were first reported in the Zone at eleven o'clock that morning, the 13th. I drove down with two of our committee members to meet them, just a small detachment at the southern entrance to the Zone. They showed no hostility, though a few moments later they killed twenty refugees who were frightened by their presence and ran from them. For it seems to be the rule here, as it was in Shanghai in 1932, that anyone who runs must be shot or bayoneted.

Meanwhile we were busy at headquarters disarming soldiers who had been unable to escape and had come into the Zone for protection. We assured them that if they gave up their equipment their lives would be spared by the Japanese. But it was a vain promise. All would have preferred to die fighting to being taken out and shot or sabred or used for bayonet practice, as they all were later on.

There was still some shellfire that day but very little that landed in the Zone. We discovered some fragments of shrapnel in our yard that evening; Dr. Wilson[1] had a narrow escape from shrapnel bits that came through the window of his operating room while he was operating; and a shell passed through one of the new University dormitories; but there were no casualties. The Communications building, the most beautiful in all Nanking, with its superb ceremonial hall, was in flames, but whether from shellfire or started by the retreating Chinese we do not know.

On Tuesday the 14th the Japanese were pouring into the city —tanks, artillery, infantry, trucks. The reign of terror commenced, and it was to increase in severity and horror with each of the succeeding ten days. They were the conquerors of China's capital, the seat of the hated Chiang Kai-shek government, and they were given free reign to do as they pleased. The proclamation on the handbills which airplanes scattered over the city saying that the Japanese were the only real friends of the Chinese and would protect the good, of course meant no more than most of their statements. And to show their 'sincerity' they raped, looted and killed at will. Men were taken from our refugee camps in droves, as we supposed at the time for labor—but they have never been heard from again, nor will they be. A colonel and his staff called at my office and spent an hour trying to learn where the "six thousand disarmed soldiers" were. Four times that day Japanese soldiers came and tried to take our cars away. Others in the meantime succeeded in stealing three of our cars that were elsewhere. On Sone's[2] they

[1] Dr. Robert O. Wilson, American, University of Nanking Hospital.
[2] Rev. Hubert L. Sone, American, Nanking Theological Seminary.

tore off the American flag, and threw it on the ground, broke a window and managed to get away all within the five minutes he had gone into Prof. Stanley's[1] house. They tried to steal our trucks—did succeed in getting two,—so ever since it has been necessary for two Americans to spend most of their time riding trucks as they delivered rice and coal. Their experience in dealing daily with these Japanese car thieves would make an interesting story in itself. And at the University Hospital they took the watches and fountain pens from the nurses.

Durdin,[2] of the *New York Times,* started for Shanghai by motor that day, though none of us had much faith he would get through. I hurriedly wrote a letter for him to take, but he was turned back at Kuyung. Steele,[3] of the *Chicago Daily News,* managed to get out to the river and reported that a number of Japanese destroyers had just arrived. A lieutenant gave him the news of the sinking of the "Panay" but had no details, nor did he mention the other ships that were sunk. After all their efforts to have us go aboard, finally leaving us with a couple of lengths of rope by which we could get down over the wall and to the river—it was ironical indeed that the "Panay" should be bombed and we still safe.

Mr. Rabe,[4] our Chairman, Nanking head of Siemens China Co., and Smythe,[5] our secretary, called at military headquarters in the hope of seeing the commanding officer and stopping the intolerable disorders but had to wait until the next day as he had not yet entered the city. Their calls were quite useless anyway.

On Wednesday I drove around to my house, which is just outside the Zone, to see if everything was all right. Yesterday the gates were intact, but today the side gate was broken in and the south door open. I had no time to investigate but asked a friendly looking major who had just moved in across the street to keep an eye on

[1] Prof. C. Stanley, American, Nanking Theological Seminary.
[2] F. Tillman Durdin, American, Nanking correspondent of the *New York Times.*
[3] Archibald T. Steele, American, Nanking correspondent of the *Chicago Daily News.*
[4] John H. D. Rabe, German, Chairman of the International Committee for the Nanking Safety Zone.
[5] Dr. Lewis S. C. Smythe, American, University of Nanking.

the place, which he promised to do. A staff officer from the Navy was waiting for me. He expressed his deep concern over the loss of the "Panay," but he too could give no details. The Navy would be glad to send a destroyer to Shanghai with any of the members of the American community who wished to go, also to send radio messages of purely a personal nature. He seemed somewhat disappointed in the brevity of the message I wrote out: "Wilbur, National Committee YMCA, Shanghai: All foreigners Nanking safe and well. Please inform interested parties."—also when I told him that with the exception of a couple of newspaper men the rest of us wished to stay in Nanking.

I offered to drive him back to his ship—he had been obliged to walk the four miles in,—but half way we were stopped by an army major who told us that no civilians were allowed further north as they were still rounding up some Chinese soldiers and it was unsafe. We happened to be beside the Ministry of War at the time and it was all too evident that an execution was going on, hundreds of poor disarmed soldiers with many innocent civilians among them—the real reason for his not wanting me to go further. So Mr. Sekiguchi of H.I.J.M.S. "Seta" had to walk the rest of the way. But that afternoon I stole a march on the surly major; I went to Hsiakwan by back roads. At the gate I was stopped, but I had Smith[1] of Reuters and Steele with me who were leaving on that destroyer, so we were finally allowed to pass. I have already described the conditions at that gate—we actually had to drive over masses of dead bodies to get through. But the scene beggars description. I shall never forget that ride.

At the jetty we found Durdin of the *Times* and Art Mencken of Paramount Films, with whom I had just made that trip to the northwest, to Shansi and Sian, already there, for they were going too, and I had promised to drive Durdin's car back to the American Embassy for him. Mr. Okamura[2] of the Japanese Embassy, just arrived from Shanghai, was also there and gave us the names of the killed and wounded on the "Panay" and the Standard Oil boats, so I offered him a lift back to the city. But at the gate we were

---
[1] L. C. Smith, British, Nanking correspondent of Reuters News Agency.
[2] Katsuze Okamura, Third Secretary of the Japanese Embassy.

stopped again, and this time the guard positively refused to let me enter. No foreigners were allowed to enter Nanking, and the fact that I had just come from there made no difference. Even Mr. Okamura's appeals were in vain—the Embassy cuts no ice with the army in Japan. The only thing to do was to wait while Okamura took one of the cars to military headquarters and sent back a special pass. It took an hour and a half; but I had the November *Reader's Digest,* the last piece of mail to reach me from the outside, with me so that time passed quickly. The stench at the gate was awful— and here and there dogs were gnawing at the corpses.

At our staff conference that evening word came that soldiers were taking all 1,300 men in one of our camps near headquarters to shoot them. We knew there were a number of ex-soldiers among them, but Rabe had been promised by an officer that very afternoon that their lives would be spared. It was now all too obvious what they were going to do. The men were lined up and roped together in groups of about a hundred by soldiers with bayonets fixed; those who had hats had them roughly torn off and thrown on the ground, —and then by the light of our headlights we watched them marched away to their doom. Not a whimper came from the entire throng. Our own hearts were lead. Were those four lads from Canton who had trudged all the way up from the south and yesterday had reluctantly given me their arms among them, I wondered; or that tall, strapping sergeant from the north whose disillusioned eyes as he made the fatal decision, still haunt me? How foolish I had been to tell them the Japanese would spare their lives! We had confidently expected that they would live up to their promises, at least in some degree, and that order would be established with their arrival. Little did we dream that we should see such brutality and savagery as has probably not been equalled in modern times. For worse days were yet to come.

The problem of transportation became acute on the 16th, with the Japanese still stealing our trucks and cars. I went over to the American Embassy where the Chinese staff were still standing by, and borrowed Mr. Atcheson's car for Mills[1] to deliver coal. For our big concentrations of refugees and our three big rice kitchens

[1] Rev. W. P. Mills, American, Northern Presbyterian Mission.

had to have fuel as well as rice. We now had twenty-five camps, ranging from two hundred to twelve thousand people in them. In the University buildings alone there were nearly thirty thousand and in Ginling College, which was reserved for women and children, the three thousand were rapidly increased to over nine thousand. In the latter place even the covered passageways between buildings were crowded, while within every foot of space was taken. We had figured on sixteen square feet to a person, but actually they were crowded in much closer than that. For while no place was safe, we did manage to preserve a fair degree of safety at Ginling, to a lesser degree in the University. Miss Vautrin,[1] Mrs. Twinem[2] and Mrs. Chen[3] were heroic in their care and protection of the women.

That morning the cases of rape began to be reported. Over a hundred women that we knew of were taken away by soldiers, seven of them from the University library; but there must have been many times that number who were raped in their homes. Hundreds were on the streets trying to find a place of safety. At tiffin time Riggs,[4] who was associate commissioner of housing, came in crying. The Japanese had emptied the Law College and Supreme Court and taken away practically all the men, to a fate we could only guess. Fifty of our policemen had been taken with them. Riggs had protested, only to be roughly handled by the soldiers and twice struck by an officer. Refugees were searched for money and anything they had on them was taken away, often to their last bit of bedding. At our staff conference at four we could hear the shots of the execution squad nearby. It was a day of unspeakable terror for the poor refugees and horror for us.

I dashed over to my house for a few minutes on the way to tiffin at Prof. Buck's[5] where I was living with six others. The two American flags were still flying and the proclamations by the Embassy still on the gates and front door; but the side gate had been smashed

[1] Miss Minnie Vautrin, American, Ginling College.
[2] Mrs. Paul DeWitt Twinem, formerly American but now a Chinese citizen, University of Nanking.
[3] Matron and Superintendent of Dormitories, Ginling College.
[4] Charles H. Riggs, American, University of Nanking.
[5] Professor J. Lossing Buck, American, University of Nanking.

and the door broken open. Within was confusion. Every drawer and closet and trunk had been opened, locks smashed. The attic was littered ankle deep. I could not stop to see what was taken but most of the bedding was gone and some clothing and food stuffs. A carved teak screen had been stripped of its embroidered panels, a gift of Dr. C. T. Wang,[1] and a heavy oak buffet battered in. Yates McDaniel[2] of the Associated Press, the last of our newspaper men, left in the afternoon by another destroyer for Shanghai. With him I sent another short letter which I hope got through.

[1] Chinese Ambassador to U.S.A.
[2] C. Yates McDaniel, American, Nanking correspondent, Associated Press of America.

CHAPTER II

ROBBERY, MURDER AND RAPE

Continuing his narrative *in diary form the writer says:*
Friday, Dec. 17. Robbery, murder, rape continue unabated. A rough estimate would be at least a thousand women raped last night and during the day. One poor woman was raped thirty-seven times. Another had her five months infant deliberately smothered by the brute to stop its crying while he raped her. Resistance means the bayonet. The hospital is rapidly filling up with the victims of Japanese cruelty and barbarity. Bob Wilson, our only surgeon, has his hands more than full and has to work into the night. Rickshas, cattle, pigs, donkeys, often the sole means of livelihood of the people, are taken from them. Our rice kitchens and rice shop are interfered with. We have had to close the latter.

After dinner I took Bates[1] to the University and McCallum[2] to the hospital where they will spend the night, then Mills and Smythe to Ginling, for one of our group has been sleeping there each night. At the gate of the latter place we were stopped by what seemed to be a searching party. We were roughly pulled from the car at the point of the bayonet, my car keys taken from me, lined up and frisked for arms, our hats jerked off, electric torches held to our faces, our passports and purpose in coming demanded. Opposite us were Miss Vautrin, Mrs. Twinem and Mrs. Chen, with a score of refugee women kneeling on the ground. The sergeant, who spoke a little French (about as much as I do), insisted there were soldiers concealed there. I maintained that aside from about fifty domestics and other members of their staff there were no men on the place. This he said he did not believe and said he would shoot

[1] Dr. M. S. Bates, American, University of Nanking.
[2] Rev. James H. McCallum, American, University of Nanking Hospital.

all he found beyond that number. He then demanded that we all leave, including the ladies, and when Miss Vautrin refused she was roughly hustled to the car. Then he changed his mind: the ladies were told to stay and we to go. We tried to insist that one of us should stay too, but this he would not permit. Altogether we were kept standing there for over an hour before we were released. The next day we learned that this gang had abducted twelve girls from the school.

Saturday, Dec. 18. At breakfast Riggs, who lives in the Zone a block away but has his meals with us, reported that two women, one a cousin of a Y.M.C.A. Secretary, were raped in his house while he was having dinner with us. Wilson reported a boy of five years of age brought to the hospital after having been stabbed with a bayonet five times, once through his abdomen; a man with eighteen bayonet wounds, a woman with seventeen cuts on her face and several on her legs. Between four and five hundred terrorized women poured into our headquarters compound in the afternoon and spent the night in the open.

Sunday, Dec. 19. A day of complete anarchy. Several big fires raging today, started by the soldiers, and more are promised. The American flag was torn down in a number of places. At the American School it was trampled on and the caretaker told he would be killed if he put it up again. The proclamations placed on all American and other foreign properties by the Japanese Embassy are flouted by their soldiers, sometimes deliberately torn off. Some houses are entered from five to ten times in one day and the poor people looted and robbed and the women raped. Several were killed in cold blood, for no apparent reason whatever. Six out of seven of our sanitation squad in one district were slaughtered; the seventh escaped, wounded, to tell the tale. Toward evening today two of us rushed to Dr. Brady's[1] house (he is away) and chased four would-be rapers out and took all the women there to the University. Sperling is busy at this game all day. I also went to the house of Douglas Jenkins[2] of our Embassy. The flag was still there;

[1] Dr. Richard F. Brady, American, Acting Superintendent of the University of Nanking Hospital.
[2] Douglas Jenkins, Jr., Third Secretary, American Embassy.

but in the garage his house boy lay dead, another servant, dead, was under a bed, both brutally killed. The house was in utter confusion. There are still many corpses on the streets. All of them civilians as far as we can see. The Red Swastika Society would bury them, but their truck has been stolen, their coffins used for bonfires, and several of their workers bearing their insignia have been marched away.

Smythe and I called again at the Japanese Embassy with a list of fifty-five additional cases of violence, all authenticated, and told Messers. Tanaka[1] and Fukui[2] that today was the worst so far. We were assured that they would 'do their best' and hoped that things would be better 'soon,' but it is quite obvious that they have little or no influence with the military whatever, and the military have no control over the soldiers. We were also told that seventeen military police had recently arrived who would help in restoring order. Seventeen for an army of perhaps fifty thousand! Yet we rather like the three men of the Embassy. They are probably doing their best. But I had to smile when they asked my help in getting cars and a mechanic for them after so many of ours had been stolen. I felt like referring them to their own military—but instead I took them around to the American Embassy and borrowed our Ambassador's and two others for them and later sent them our Russian repair man.

Monday, Dec. 20. Vandalism and violence continue absolutely unchecked. Whole sections of the city are being systematically burned. At 5 p.m. Smythe and I went for a drive. All Taiping Road, the most important shopping street in the city, was in flames. We drove through showers of sparks and over burning embers. Further south we could see the soldiers inside the shops setting fire to them and still further they were loading the loot into army trucks. Next, to the Y.M.C.A.—and it was in flames, evidently fired only a hour or so ago. The surrounding buildings were as yet untouched. I hadn't the heart to watch it, so we hurried on. That night I counted fourteen fires from my window, some of them covering considerable areas.

[1] Sueo Tanaka, Attaché, Japanese Embassy (now Consul).
[2] Kiyoshi Fukui, Japanese Consul-General, Nanking.

Our group here at the house drafted a message to the American Consulate-General in Shanghai asking that diplomatic representatives be sent here immediately as the situation was urgent, then asked the Japanese Embassy to send it via navy radio. Needless to say it was never sent.

Tuesday, Dec. 21. Fourteen of us called on Tanaka at 2.30 and presented a letter signed by all twenty-two foreigners protesting the burning of the city and continued disorders. More promises! Rabe fears for his house, for buildings are burning across the street from him. He has over four hundred refugees living in matsheds in his garden. The problem of feeding is becoming serious—some refugees, hungry, started rioting in the University. Our coal will soon be finished, but Riggs is scouting for more. The Japanese have sealed all supplies of coal and rice. Soldiers came into our place today, over the wall, and tried to take our cars while we were all out, and at another time they nearly got Sone's truck from him. Rabe had a letter today from Dr. Rosen of the German Embassy, through Mr. Tanaka, saying he was on the H.M.S. "Bee" at Hsiakwan but not allowed to land and asking about German properties. Rabe replied that he was glad to be able to inform him that two houses were not looted, the Ambassador's and his own, and that two cars were still left! (There are over fifty German residences in Nanking.)

Wednesday, Dec. 22. Firing squad at work very near us at 5 a.m. today. Counted over a hundred shots. The University was entered twice during the night, the policeman at the gate held up at the point of a bayonet, and a door broken down. The Japanese military police recently appointed to duty there were asleep. Representatives of the new Japanese police called and promised order by January 1. They also asked for the loan of motorcars and trucks. Went with Sperling to see fifty corpses in some ponds a quarter of a mile east of headquarters. All obviously civilians, hands bound behind backs, one with the top half of his head cut completely off. Were they used for sabre practice? On the way home for tiffin stopped to help the father of a Y.M.C.A. writer who was being threatened by a drunken soldier with the bayonet, the poor mother frantic with fear, and before sitting down had to run over with two of our fellows to chase soldiers out of Gee's[1] and Daniel's[2] houses, where they were just about to rape the women. We had to laugh to see those brave soldiers trying to get over a barbed wire fence as we chased them!

Bates and Riggs had to leave before they were through tiffin to chase soldiers out of the Sericulture building—several drunk. And on my arrival at office there was an S.O.S. call, which Rabe and I answered, from Sperling and Kroeger who were seriously threatened by a drunk with a bayonet. By fortunate chance Tanaka of the Embassy together with some general arrived at the same moment. The soldier had his face soundly slapped a couple of times by the general but I don't suppose he got any more than that. We have heard of no cases of discipline so far. If a soldier is caught by an officer or M.P. he is very politely told that he shouldn't do that again. In the evening I walked home with Riggs after dinner—a woman of fifty-four had been raped in his house just before our arrival. It's cruel to leave the women to their fate, but of course it is impossible for us to spend all our time protecting them. Mr. Wu, engineer in the power plant which is located in Hsiakwan, brought us the amusing news that forty-three of the fifty-four employees who had so heroically kept the plant going to the very last day and had finally been obliged to seek refuge in the International Export Company, a British factory on the river front, had been taken out and shot on the ground that the power plant was a government concern—which it is not. Japanese officials have been at my office daily trying to get hold of these very men so they could start the turbines and have electricity. It was small comfort to be able to tell them that their own military had murdered most of them.

Thursday, Dec. 23. Sone was the one to get mishandled today. At Stanley Smith's house he found an officer and soldier who had just removed the American flag, also the Japanese proclamation, forced the refugee living there out, and said they must use the place

[1] C. T. Gee, Chinese, resident architect and engineer, University of Nanking.
[2] Dr. J. H. Daniel, American, Superintendent, University of Nanking Hospital.

as a registration centre. He must have had a pretty uncomfortable time of it, for he was finally forced to sign a paper giving them the right to use the place for two weeks. And Sone is not a man to take things lying down! A protest to the Embassy finally got the soldiers out of the place. Seventy were taken from our camp at the Rural Leaders' Training School and shot. No system—soldiers seize anyone they suspect. Calluses on hands are proof that the man was a soldier, a sure death warrant. Ricksha coolies, carpenters and other laborers are frequently taken. At noon a man was led to headquarters with head burned cinder black—eyes and ears gone, nose partly, a ghastly sight. I took him to the hospital in my car where he died a few hours later. His story was that he was one of a gang of some hundred who had been tied together, then gasoline thrown over them and set afire. He happened to be on the outer edge so got the gas only over his head. Later another similar case was brought to the hospital with more extensive burns. He also died. It seems probable that they were first machine-gunned but not all killed. The first man had no wounds but the second did. Still later I saw a third with similar head and arm burns lying at the corner of the road to my house, opposite the Drum Tower. Evidently he had managed to struggle that far before dying. Incredible brutality!

Friday, Dec. 24. A Chinese at the U.S. Embassy reports that the Chinese staff and their relatives, living in the Embassy, were all robbed last night by an officer and his men; Paston's office door was bayoneted, three cars stolen from the compound and two more this morning. Later I had the pleasure of telling Tanaka that Mencken's car, which I had promised him the use of yesterday, was among those stolen. Registration of Chinese started today. The military say there are still twenty thousand soldiers in the Zone and that they must get rid of these 'monsters.' I question if there are a hundred left. Anyway, many more innocent must suffer and all are fearful and nervous. The Chinese Self-Government Committee, formed day before yesterday at the invitation of Tanaka, may be helpful in this; but there are spies already at work. We caught one here. I just saved him from a bad beating, so locked him up in our basement and later turned him over to the Chinese police. What will they do to him? Strangle him I suppose—but I have told them to be careful! Constant interference from the Japanese today: more of our sanitary squad taken, also the policeman at the University gate, and they are constantly trying to get our trucks. They also sealed up one of our coal depots but Riggs finally managed to talk them out of that.

Christmas Eve. Kroeger,[1] Sperling and Dr. Trimmer[2] in for dinner with us—a good dinner, too, with roast beef and sweet potatoes. Rabe did not dare to leave his house as Japanese soldiers come over his wall many times a day. He always makes them leave by the same way they come instead of by the gate, and when any of them objects he thrusts his Nazi armband in their face and points to his Nazi decoration, the highest in the country, and asks them if they know what that means. It always works! He joined us later in the evening and gave each of us a beautiful leather-bound Siemens diary. We sang Christmas songs with Wilson at the piano.

Christmas Day. A perfect day too, as far as weather is concerned. And conditions also seem slightly better. There were crowds on the streets with quite a number of stalls selling things. But at tiffin time, while we were sitting at roast goose, with Miss Vautrin, Miss Bauer,[3] Miss Blanche Wu,[4] and Miss Pearl Bromley Wu[5] as our guests, we had to answer three calls for help and then turn soldiers out of Fenn's[6] and the Chinese faculty house and the Sericulture building. That day the American flag was taken from the Rural Leaders' Training School; seven soldiers spent that night and the night before in the Bible Teachers' Training School and raped the women, a girl of twelve was raped by three soldiers

---

[1] Christian Kroeger, German, Representative of Carlowitz & Company.

[2] Dr. C. S. Trimmer, American, Acting Superintendent, University of Nanking Hospital.

[3] Miss Grace Bauer, American, University of Nanking Hospital.

[4] Miss Blanche Wu, Chinese, Instructor in the Department of Biology, Ginling College.

[5] Miss Pearl Bromley Wu, Chinese, adopted daughter of Mr. and Mrs. Charles L. Bromley, formerly of the American Baptist Foreign Mission Society.

[6] Dr. Wm. P. Fenn, American, University of Nanking.

almost next door to us and another of thirteen, before we could send relief. There were also more bayonet cases; Wilson reports that of the 240 cases in the hospital three-quarters are due to Japanese violence since the occupation. At the University, registration commenced. The people were told that if any ex-soldiers were there and would step out, they would be used in the labor corps and their lives would be saved. About 240 stepped out. They were herded together and taken away. Two or three lived to tell the tale and, by feigning death after they were wounded, escaped and came to the hospital. One group was machine-gunned, another was surrounded by soldiers and used for bayonet practice. We have had quite a number of cases where men have faced the execution squad, escaped with only a wound or two, perhaps lying all day and into the night covered by the corpses of their comrades to escape detection, and then getting to the hospital or to friends. A rash bit of carelessness on the part of the Japanese!

Monday, Dec. 27. The third week of Japanese occupation begins and is celebrated with the arrival of a Nisshin Kisen Kaisha ship from Shanghai. Four representatives of the company called at my office and promised that a regular service will soon be established on the river. A number of ladies are in the party and are taken on a sight-seeing trip of the city. They distribute a few sweets to some children and seem tremendously pleased with themselves, also with Japan's wonderful victory, but of course they hear nothing of the real truth—nor does the rest of the world, I suppose. The soldiers are still completely out of control, there is no co-operation between the Army and the Embassy. The Army even refuse to recognize the new Self-Government Committee which was called into being by the Embassy, and its members are deliberately slighted. They are told that they are a conquered people and should expect no favors. Our list of instances of disorders and cruelty keeps mounting and those we never hear of must be many, many times what are reported or observed. A few of today's: A boy of thirteen, taken by the Japanese nearly two weeks ago, beaten with an iron rod and then bayoneted because he didn't do his work satisfactorily. A car with an officer and two soldiers came to the University last night, raped three women on the premises and took away one with them. The Bible Teachers' Training School was entered many times; people were robbed and twenty women raped. The hospital night superintendent was taken by soldiers in spite of Miss Bauer's protests. The burning of the city continues, and today two of the Christian Mission School buildings in the south part of the city were fired, also Kiessling & Bader's[1] (German). But Takatama, Chief of the Embassy police, calls and now promises protection for all foreign buildings and starts out with Sperling to inspect German properties. Personally I think he is promising far more than he can deliver. What a list of claims Japan will have presented to her— and it all seems so utterly needless—for there are hundreds of foreign properties in Nanking almost all of which have been looted by her soldiers. And the cars that they have stolen. I think I forgot to mention that yesterday Smythe and I called at the British Embassy which is in the far-north-western part of the city, out of the Zone. All the cars, eleven of them, had been taken away by soldiers, also a couple of trucks, but fortunately the servants had fared fairly well. Every block or so one now sees abandoned cars—and batteries and anything else useful—left where they are, usually overturned.

There was one bright spot today, though, and that was the arrival by the N.K.K. boat, through the Japanese Embassy, of a letter to me from Dr. Fong See[2]—the first and only letter to come to any of us in all these past three or four weeks. He wanted to know if we might not be in need of funds for our relief work and offered to hold some of the money that was coming in in response to our appeal through Rotary International. That's Fong all over! And we'll need additional funds all right—many many thousands. I have a nightmare every time I think of what we'll soon be needing; for where are we going to get it?

Tuesday, Dec. 28. What we had feared—bad weather: A steady drizzle and then snow. The poor refugees living in huts, many no

[1] A well-known bakery and confectionery, situated in the main shopping district.
[2] Dr. Fong Foo-see, American-educated, former head of the Department of English, The Commercial Press, now Governor of 81st District (Far East) Rotary International Clubs.

longer than a pup tent, will have a miserable time of it, for most of these huts are not rainproof. And then there is the sticky mud. But we have certainly been fortunate in having had ideal weather up to this. I inspected some of our camps today. The crowding in most of them is terrible and of course it is impossible to keep them clean. Our camp managers and their assistants, all volunteer workers, are doing a splendid job on the whole in maintaining discipline, feeding the people and keeping things fairly sanitary. But how long must we maintain these camps? When are the people going to be permitted to return to their homes—those who have any homes left? When will order ever be established?

I went over to the School today for the first time. It is located not far beyond my residence. Everything had been turned upside down and many of the instruments in the physics laboratory deliberately smashed. On the athletic field was a dead cow, half eaten by the dogs. The Embassy proclamation had been torn from the gate.

Wednesday, Dec. 29. Weather better today, fortunately. Registration continues, most inefficiently, and the people are given no information as to where and when to appear. More taken as ex-soldiers. Women and old men come kneeling and crying, begging our help in getting back their husbands and sons. In a few cases we have been successful, but the military resent any interference from us. Word comes through from Hsiakwan by a representative of the Chinese Red Cross Society that there are approximately twenty thousand refugees along the river front. The supply of rice we let them have before the Japanese arrived is nearly exhausted and there is great suffering. They ask to come into the Safety Zone, but we are already too crowded. Anyway, the Japanese wouldn't permit it, nor will they permit us to go out there and render help. For the time being they will have to get along as best they can.

Guards are at last posted at the various foreign embassies. But why wasn't it done two weeks ago? Our homes are still left unprotected; and the few guards posted at some of our camps are often more of a nuisance than a help. They demand fire and food, beds and often other things of the people.

ROBBERY, MURDER AND RAPE

Thursday, Dec. 30. I called in the servants today, eighteen of them, paid them up to the 15th of next month and told them that they must now try to find other work. It was a hard job. Some of them have been with us for many years and are fine, faithful fellows. W. and I hope it may be possible to start something in a small way in the old school buildings if and when we get order established, but few of our members are left and it will be a difficult matter to build up a new constituency from the material that is now in Nanking. W. has done a splendid job as assistant housing commissioner, and so has C. as one of the camp superintendents, while our servants have all been doing their bit in one way or another.

When I called at the Japanese Embassy this afternoon they were busy giving instructions to about sixty Chinese, most of them our camp managers, on how New Year was to be celebrated. The old five-barred flag is to replace the Nationalist flag, and they were told to make a thousand of these and also a thousand Japanese flags for that event. Camps of over a thousand must have twenty representatives present, smaller camps ten. At one o'clock New Year's Day the five-barred flag is to be raised above the Drum Tower, there will be 'suitable' speeches and 'music' (according to the programme) and of course moving pictures will be taken of the happy people waving flags, and welcoming the new regime. In the meantime the burning of the city continues, three cases of girls of twelve and thirteen years of age being raped or abducted are reported; Sperling has a busy time chasing soldiers out of houses in the immediate vicinity of headquarters; the Sericulture building (a part of the University of Nanking—American property) has a cordon thrown round it while soldiers engage in a man hunt, etc. etc.

Friday, Dec. 31. A comparatively quiet day. For the first time no cases of violence were reported for the night. The Japanese are busy with their New Year preparations. Two days of holiday are announced. We dread them, for it means more drunken soldiers. Refugees are advised to stay indoors. Rabe invited our household to his house after dinner and lighted his Christmas tree for us, and each of us received a New Year's card with our Zone emblem—a circle with a cross within it in red—signed by all twenty-two of the foreign community in Nanking. He also entertained with stories of some of his experiences in South Africa. On his walls hang some magnificent trophies of his hunts. *New Year's Eve!* Thoughts of home and loved ones come crowding in. What wouldn't one give for a letter from 'home'! Evidently we are going to have to exercise patience a while longer, for the Japanese Embassy tells us that it will still be weeks before the postal services are re-established here. They also tell us that it will be a month at least before any of us is allowed to leave the city on a visit to Shanghai. We are virtually prisoners here!

There is perhaps no purpose to be served by going further with this story and telling of acts of horror that have been committed since. It is now the 11th of January, and while conditions are vastly improved there has not been a day that has not had its atrocities, some of them of a most revolting nature. With the arrival on the 6th of three representatives of the American Embassy and on the 9th of three of both the British and German Embassies we feel a little more assurance that conditions will still further improve. But only last night I drove past four new fires that had just been started and saw soldiers within a shop just starting a fifth. There has not been a day since Dec. 19 that fires have not been started by Japanese soldiers. And Kroeger, who managed to slip out of the East Gate the other day, tells us that all the villages as far as he went, some twenty miles, are burned and that not a living Chinese or farm animal is to be seen.

We are at last in touch with the outside world through the radio, and that is a great blessing; for last Sunday I got our house connected up and we now have electricity. At our Committee Headquarters we had current a few days earlier. Only the Japanese are supposed to have electricity, though, so we are not advertising the fact. Then we have seen a couple of issues of a Shanghai Japanese paper and two of the Tokyo *Nichi Nichi*. These tell us that even as early as Dec. 28 the stores were rapidly opening up and business returning to normal, that the Japanese were cooperating with us in feeding the poor refugees, that the city had been cleared of *Chinese* looters, and that peace and order now reigned! We'd be tempted to laugh if it all wasn't so tragic.

I have written this account in no spirit of vindictiveness. War is brutalizing, especially a war of conquest, and it would seem to me from my experiences in this, as also in the Shanghai 'war' of 1932, that the Japanese army, with no background of Christian idealism, has today become a brutal, destructive force that not only menaces the East but also may some day menace the West, and that the world should know the truth about what is happening. How this situation should be dealt with I shall have to leave with abler minds than mine to consider.

There is a bright side in this story, of course, and that is the wonderful spirit of service that has been shown by our Chinese and foreign friends alike and the intimate fellowship we have enjoyed in our common cause. Our hearts have been frequently warmed, too, by the innumerable times the refugees have expressed appreciation for what we have tried to do; and our own losses and inconveniences seem so trivial when compared with what they have suffered. Then our three German friends on the Committee have won both our admiration and affection. They have been a tower of strength—without them I don't see how we would have got through.

What of the future? The immediate future is anything but bright, but the Chinese have an unsurpassed capacity for suffering and endurance, besides their many other qualities, and right must triumph in the end. Anyway, I shall always be glad that I threw in my lot with them.

A selection of case reports covering this period will be found in Appendix A.

CHAPTER III

PROMISE AND PERFORMANCE

Towards the end *of December the Japanese authorities made known their intention of carrying out the registration of all the thirty thousand odd refugees concentrated at the University of Nanking, an American missionary institution founded fifty years ago. The registration was made of all residents in the city. The following account of what happened was written by a foreign member of the University faculty on January 25 from a draft of information prepared on December 31 and notes made on January 3:*

Registration was begun on December 20 in the main compound, occupied mainly by women. To the relatively small number of men there, the military authorities added more than two thousand from the new Library. Out of the total of about three thousand men massed together on the tennis courts below Swazey Hall, between two and three hundred stepped out in answer to a half-hour of haranguing to this effect: "All who have been soldiers or who have performed compulsory labor (*fu juh*) pass to the rear. Your lives will be spared, and you will be given work if you thus voluntarily come forth. If you do not, and upon inspection you are discovered, you will be shot." Short speeches were repeated many times over by Chinese under the instructions of Japanese officers. They were Chinese who wished to save as many of their people as possible from the fate that others had met as former soldiers or as men accused wrongfully of being former soldiers. The speeches were clearly and thoroughly heard by Mr. H. L. Sone, Mr. Charles H. Riggs, and myself, as well as by many Chinese members of the University staff. It was thought by some Chinese that certain men who stepped out were influenced by fear or by misunderstanding of the term for compulsory labor. Assuredly, a fair number of them had never been soldiers.

PROMISE AND PERFORMANCE

The actual conduct of the registration was in the hands of officers whom we later came to know as relatively considerate and reasonable, though that is no praise for, nor exemption from, the responsibility they must bear for the actions of their men in open daylight and in public view, even during the process of registration while the officers were present. At the outset that morning, the chief officer asked my permission to conduct the registration on American property, a deference most startling in the experience of Japanese occupation. Moreover, he and others took especial pains to avoid causing unnecessary fear at the beginning, and I am inclined to credit them with sincerity of intention. Again, although the soldiers sorted out for examination nearly one thousand from the remaining men, including those who had not stepped out, the officers permitted all but one of these thousand to be released for registration upon the casual 'guarantees' given by various Chinese as the line was marched by for individual inspection: and that one was let go upon the joint representations of Mr. Sone and myself. Furthermore, officers before noon asked that we provide two meals of rice for each of the two to three hundred "volunteers" to be replaced by rice from military stores. Even the common soldiers acting as guards were fairly kind, and gave out more cigarettes than blows. In the afternoon the men reported individually their names and occupations, which were written down.

Meanwhile another element had been introduced. Two additional officers, with higher status at least for this particular job, came in. One of them was violent in his dissatisfaction with what had been done. This man had shown gross roughness and stupidity during a visit to the University on the previous day, and we were often to encounter his evil doings and coarse methods as head of the military police for this district. Toward five o'clock in the afternoon, the two or three hundred men who had stepped out were taken away in two groups by military police. One of them in retrospect declared that he was beginning to be suspicious of the unusual courtesy of some of the friendly guards.

Next morning a man with five bayonet wounds came to the University Hospital. On two occasions before this man declared with fair clarity that he had been a refugee in the library of the University. He stated that he had been picked up by the Japanese on the street and added to a group that had come from the tennis courts mentioned above. That evening, he said, somewhere to the west, about 130 Japanese soldiers had killed most of five hundred similar captives with bayonet thrusts. When he regained consciousness he found that the Japanese had gone, and managed to crawl away during the night. He was not familiar with this part of Nanking, and was vague as to places.

On the morning of the 27th another man was brought to me. He said that he was one of thirty or forty who had escaped the death met by most of the two hundred or three hundred taken away the previous evening. The man desired help for himself and one or more companions in the registration then continuing, but since I was surrounded by military police at the time, I had to tell him that registration was that day limited to women, and that it was best not to speak further at the moment. Three times later I inquired for this group, but I heard nothing more of them.

In the course of the same day and the next (27th and 28th) I heard and checked apparently circumstantial reports that part of the men taken away had been bound in groups of five and ten, to be passed successively from a first room of a large house into a second room or court where there was a big fire. As each group went forward, groans and cries could be heard by the remainder, but no shots. Some twenty remaining from an original sixty broke away in desperation through a back wall and made their escape. Part of the detachment brought from the University were said to have been saved by the pleas of priests living in the neighborhood (Wu T'ai Shan, clearly specified in all this group of indirect reports, which came in part from Buddhists). A similar story had been heard by Mr. Riggs early in the evening of the 26th, conjecturally too soon to come from the same incident. This confusion or complexity of reports was discouraging, and several attempts at further inquiry met with little result while other duties and problems pressed upon us each day.

On the 31st, two men gave a request for aid, with their story, to a trusted assistant of the Library refugee camp, who offered to bring them to me for confirmation if desired. One frankly declared that he had been a soldier, thus creating some presumption in favor of his truthfulness. They declared that the two hundred-three hundred men from the University were split up into various groups. They themselves were taken first to Wu T'ai Shan, then to the bank of the canal outside Han Hsi Men where a machine gun was turned upon them. They fell, one of them wounded, among the dead men and smeared with their blood.

On the 3rd, of January, an interview was secured with two men among five acquaintances in the Library, who were survivors of the experience of December 26. One of them was in the first group taken from the University, and confirmed circumstantially the room-find-fire account at Wu T'ai Shan as given above under the date of the 27th and 28th. He estimated that of his group eighty were killed and forty to fifty escaped; one of them, wounded by a bayonet thrust, was in the Library, and could be brought to report the same facts.

The second was an unusually intelligent man, clear and specific both in narrative and under cross-questioning. He was taken with the second group to a large house at Wu T'ai Shan opposite a temple (this side has been identified with considerable assurance as one of two buildings on Shanghai Road or an alley from it, across from the American School a short distance to the south). There on the road he was alarmed by noticing Chinese priests and a Japanese priest sorrowfully praying and putting long strips of paper at the entrance to the temple. (Since the report of a Japanese priest in Nanking was an utter novelty, I sceptically asked how he knew that the priest was Japanese. The informant replied that his footgear was cleft for a separate big toe; and later I learned that the informant had lived in Tientsin, where he would naturally acquire such recognition. A few days later I myself saw such a priest on Shanghai Road.) Sensing that the atmosphere was ominous, the man spoke to a guard who had been friendly, indicating his anxiety. The guard silently wrote in the dirt with a stick, *ta jen ming ling*—"orders from a superior."

The men in the immediate vicinity of my informant (he did not speak of others) were bound with wire, wrist to wrist, in pairs. Thirty or more were taken to Han Chung Men and across the canal, where four or five in desperation broke from the column in the dusk or dark, taking advantage of protecting walls, and found a hiding-place. The man guessed by the moon that it was about one o'clock when he heard despairing cries not far to the north. At day-break he went a little in that direction and saw bodies in rows, bayoneted. Though in great fear, he managed to get past the gate safely and slip back to the Safety Zone.

To the account of this man and his testimony must be added two items. A responsible worker in the Chinese Red Cross requested us to go outside the Han Chung Men to inspect a large number of bodies there. Mr. Kroeger of the International Committee told me that he observed these bodies himself, in the course of an early venture outside the gate; but that they could not be seen from the City Wall. The gate is now closed. Burial gangs report three thousand bodies at the point, left in rows or piles after mass executions. The original informant talked so freely to me because he had a premonition of trouble during registration, which he was about to attempt. On January 7, I believe, he was one of some ten men sorted out by the military police from the men passing before them during the open registration resumed on the University compound. During that week the officers who did the actual work seemed to be under instructions to get about that many men per day, or perhaps to feel that they could satisfy their superiors with nothing less. (Naturally the voluntary admission of previous military service had practically ceased, and the whole procedure of registration had changed greatly from the earlier times.) As usual, I tried to watch these performances with some closeness, and to give a little help so far as the personnel and temper of the military would permit in each shifting hour. Failing in indirect efforts after I observed that this man was among the ten, I searched for a chance and took the best of the officers there with me, claiming (with some stretch for which I hope to be forgiven) that I recognized the man and one other who looked most promising of the remainder, and should like the favor of guaranteeing them. The second was released, but not my acquaintance, for reasons unfathomable; and further efforts brought such a kick-back that I had to desist for fear of injury to others. Death was the probable outcome though not certainly so.

Two other men from the University Library reported indirectly that they escaped from a large body of several hundred who were bayoneted along the canal wall to the north, near to San Chia Ho.

Finally, it should be remembered that this incident is only one of a series of similar acts that had been going on for two weeks, with changes on the main theme of mass murder of men accused rightfully or wrongfully of being ex-soldiers. This is not the place to discuss the dictum of international law that the lives of prisoners are to be preserved except under serious military necessity, nor the Japanese setting aside of that law for frankly stated vengeance upon persons accused of having killed in battle comrades of the troops now occupying Nanking. Other incidents involved larger numbers of men than did this one. Evidences from burials indicate that close to forty thousand unarmed persons were killed within and near the walls of Nanking, of whom some 30 per cent had never been soldiers. My special interest in these circumstances is twofold: first, because of the gross treachery of the terms by which men were made to bring themselves forward to death: second, because of the painfully close connection of our property, personnel, and protégées (refugees) with various stages of this tremendous crime. Also, the total evidence for the methods, place, and time of murder is more abundant than for some other cases in which large bodies of men were taken off never to return, but about which we have only scraps of information. It seems a clear conclusion that a large majority of the men taken from the University were murdered the same night, some of them after being mixed with groups collected from other places.

Even in all the brutality of the past weeks, it is still difficult for me to pass those tennis courts. To deal, for a number of days, with officers and soldiers who played varying parts in the drama, having to show smiles and deference for the sake of the welfare of the tens of thousands brought to the University for registration, was torture. One feels that one has become a partner with one's own Christian institution in the murder of two hundred men and so responsible for the wretched dependents if they could be found in all the surrounding sea of misery.

The officers and soldiers? Some of them were humane in comparison with violent gangs that we have faced, and many of them must have wives and children to whom they are kindly.

CHAPTER IV

THE NIGHTMARE CONTINUES

A SURVEY OF THE *situation as it presented itself nearly a month after the Japanese occupation is given in the following letter, written on January 10 by the same foreigner whose earlier account is given at the beginning of Chapter I. (See pages* 18–20.)

DEAR FRIENDS:

A few hasty jottings amid rape and bayonet stabs and reckless shooting, to be sent on the first foreign boat available since the situation developed after the Japanese entry—a U. S. Navy tug engaged in salvage work on the "Panay." Friends in Shanghai will pick this up from the Consulate-General, and will get it away somehow on a foreign boat without censorship.

Things have eased a good deal since New Year's within the crowded Safety Zone, largely through the departure of the main hordes of soldiers. "Restoration of discipline" very scrappy indeed, and even the military police have raped and robbed and ignored their duties. A new turn may come at any moment through fresh arrivals or vacillations in action. There is no policy visible. At last foreign diplomats have been allowed to re-enter (this week), which seems to indicate a desire for stabilization.

More than ten thousand[1] unarmed persons have been killed in cold blood. Most of my trusted friends would put the figure much higher. These were Chinese soldiers who threw down their arms or surrendered after being trapped; and civilians recklessly shot and bayoneted, often without even the pretext that they were soldiers, including not a few women and children. Able German colleagues put the cases of rape at twenty thousand. I should say not

[1] This figure shows the caution of the observer in making this earlier estimate, which should be compared with the subsequent evidences from burials indicating forty thousand. Cf. Chap. III, p. 51.

less than eight thousand, and it might be anywhere above that. On University property alone, including some of our staff families and the houses of Americans now occupied by Americans, I have details of more than one hundred cases and assurance of some three hundred. You can scarcely imagine the anguish and terror. Girls as low as eleven and women as old as fifty-three have been raped on University property alone. In other groups of refugees are women of seventy-two and seventy-six years of age who were raped mercilessly. On the Seminary Compound seventeen soldiers raped one woman successively in broad daylight. In fact, about one-third of the cases are in the daytime.

Practically every building in the city has been robbed repeatedly by soldiers, including the American, British and German Embassies or Ambassadors' residences, and a high percentage of all foreign property. Vehicles of all sorts, food, clothing, bedding, money, watches, some rugs and pictures, miscellaneous valuables, are the main things sought. This still goes on, especially outside the zone. There is not a store in Nanking, save the International Committee's rice shop and a military store. Most of the shops after free-for-all breaking and pilfering were systematically stripped by gangs of soldiers working with trucks, often under the observed direction of officers, and then burned. We still have several fires a day. Many sections of houses have also been burned deliberately. We have several samples of the chemical strips used by soldiers for this purpose, and have inspected all phases of the process.

Most of the refugees were robbed of their money and at least part of their scanty clothing and bedding and food. That was an utterly heartless performance, resulting in despair on every face for the first week or ten days. You can imagine the outlook for work and life in this city with shops and tools gone, no banks or communications as yet, some important blocks of houses burned out, everything else plundered and now open to cold and starving people. Some 250,000 are here, almost all in the Safety Zone and fully 100,000 entirely dependent on the International Committee for food and shelter. Others scraping along on tiny holdovers of rice and the proceeds of direct or indirect looting. Japanese supply departments are beginning to let out for monetary and political reasons a little of the rice confiscated from considerable Chinese Government supplies, though the soldiers burned not small reserves. But what next? When I asked Japanese officials about post and telegraph services, they said, "There is no plan."

The International Committee has been a great help, with a story little short of miraculous. . . . A Dane and three Englishmen aided a good deal in the preliminary stages, but were pulled out by their companies and Governments before the Chinese retired from Nanking. So the bulk of the work has fallen on American missionaries, only nine of whom have been outside the confining strain of the Hospital filled with bullet and bayonet cases; and of course some of us have had varying duties and conceptions of duty. Naturally there has been considerable Chinese aid and cooperation from the beginning, and most of the detail has had to be done by and through Chinese. Yet at some stages nothing could move, not even one truck of rice, without the actual presence of a foreigner willing to stand up to a gun when necessary. We have taken some big risks and some heavy wallops (literally as well as figuratively), but have been allowed to get away with far more than the situation seems to permit. We have blocked many robberies, persuaded or bluffed many contingents of soldiers away from rape and intended rape, besides all the general work of feeding, sheltering, negotiation, protecting and protesting after sticking our eyes and noses into everything that has gone on. It is no wonder that a Japanese Embassy officer told us the generals were angry at having to complete their occupation under the eyes of neutral observers, claiming (ignorantly, of course) that never in the history of the world has that been true before.

Sometimes we have failed cold, but the percentage of success is still big enough to justify considerable effort. We must recognize that although in some points the relationship is far from satisfactory, we have gained a good deal by the effort of the Japanese Embassy to put cushions between the Army and foreign interests, the relative decency of their Consular Police (few and not altogether angelic), and by the fact that the main figures of the enterprise have been Germans of the Berlin-Tokyo axis and Americans to be appeased after the barbarous attacks on American ships. The Japanese refused twice to send out for us a mild request for the return of American officials, because of the great number of property cases and flag problems; and even with this week's improvement we are still in practical isolation even from the countryside and riverfront, except for the opportunities of American naval wireless through the Embassy for a limited scope of messages.

No mail since about December 1, and that most tardy. Electric light in our house last night by special arrangement (seven Americans, among whom were personal links to the staff of the power plant). Japanese shot forty-three of the fifty-four technical men on the staff, falsely accusing them of being Government employees. Bombing, shelling and fires on top of that, and you can imagine that utilities are slow in resumption. But insecurity of workmen and their families was the main stumbling-block at that. Water depends on electric pumps, but we are beginning to get a trickle at low levels of the city. No dreams of telephone or bus or even ricksha. The Zone is about two square miles in area, not all built up. In this concentration we have had no accidental fire of notice, and practically no crime or violence except that of soldiers, until this present week's turning to loot outside the area in open buildings —especially for fuel. No armed police.

The University has thirty thousand refugees on various parts of its property. Problems of administration are fearful, even on the low scale of living that can be maintained. We have very few indeed of regular University staff and servants, most of whom have done splendid work. There are many volunteer helpers hastily got together by the International Committee, who have come with considerable adulteration of motives. Now we must add delation and the intimidation and purchase of agents by the Japanese. I'm in three hot spots right now over this sort of business, and begin to wonder whether they are out to get me or the University into a corner. For instance, the two occurring in the past three days involve a contradiction of my report of losses for the University's Middle School (thus putting me down for lying and cheating to the Japanese, and striking between me and a key man in that tremendous refugee camp); and a severe shove through the gate by a terrible military police officer when I tried to inquire about a good-spirited interpreter whom they had carried off bound as for death (after he had refused to leave the Middle School camp to accept their offers or submit to their threats). Incidentally, police from that office last night took a woman from a University house and raped her thoroughly, after putting a bayonet against our man Riggs, when he happened along at the wrong time. So you get a little of the flavor of our daily diet while struggling to do something for these wretched but remarkably durable and cheerful people.

The real military police numbered seventy at the time that over fifty thousand soldiers were turned loose on Nanking, and for days we never saw one. Eventually soldiers were given special armbands and called police, which means that they have special preserves for their own misdeeds, and keep out some of the ordinary run. We have seen men scolded for being caught by officers in the act of rape, and let go without penalty; others made to salute an officer following robbery. One motorized raid on the University at night was actually conducted by officers themselves, who pinned our watchman to the wall and raped three women refugees before carrying off one of them (another was a girl twelve years old).

L. had every reason to think I was finished or wounded on the "Panay," for my messages about remaining in Nanking had not got through to her and the papers in Tokyo implied that all foreigners were taken on the boats. But after forty-eight hours of distress she read in a Japanese paper an interview that a couple of dumb-bells got out of me shortly after the Japanese entry. The paper responded to the thanks of her friends by rushing out reporters and a photographer on the 17th. (Entry on 13th: "Panay" sinking on 12th, reported slowly). One of their men brought me a picture and a letter New Year's Day, the latter of course dutifully read in the Japanese Embassy. Thus we were saved a good deal of prolonged concern. I have had no other word since November 8 save that letter, although she wrote and wired many times by all sorts of routes and agencies. On December 17 she expected to come to Shanghai the first week of January, but I have heard nothing more. Perhaps a recent radio through the newly arrived gunboat will get some information from Shanghai.

However, I am not allowed to pass through a Nanking gate,

and she would not be allowed to start west of Shanghai even if means of communication were open to her. How long this state will continue we do not know. Chinese have been greatly afraid lest Americans or all foreigners would be expelled from Nanking, but *they* seem more afraid to have us go than to have us stay—so far. Meanwhile I try to keep on friendly terms with the Embassy staff and a few Japanese in semiofficial posts, and even with a few of the less violent and treacherous of the police and soldiers. But it's hard going. Four weeks today! The shells and bombs were almost comfortable, if we had only known it. And what's ahead?

PS. The disorder of this letter corresponds to that outside. I should have said at the start that the Chinese armies in an ill-conceived military program burned many villages and blocks of houses outside the wall, and did some casual looting of shops and houses for food. Otherwise they caused little trouble, though there was great anxiety over their obvious collapse, their preparations for street fighting that never occurred, and their possible injuring of the civilian population. The Chinese failure was disgraceful in the flight of high officers, and in its lack of military coordination and determination. But comparatively considered, the ordinary soldiers were very decent.

It is hardly necessary to say that this letter is not written to stir up animosity against the Japanese people. If the facts speak of needless savagery on the part of a modern army, one that covers its crimes with lying propaganda, let them speak. To me the big thing is the unmeasured misery from this war of conquest, misery multiplied by licence and stupidity, and projected far into a gloomy future."

Written a week later, the following letter is less factual than the preceding accounts but it is nevertheless valuable because of the atmosphere it conveys:

Nanking, China,
January 16, 1938

Things have happened since you left Nanking. Our school closed, the teachers and students scattered to places of safety—or relative safety, and those who remained prepared for what was to come.

We all expected a certain amount of confusion especially from the Chinese troops who would inevitably be withdrawing, and, what we feared, looting during that time. The Safety Zone was established and people moved into it from all over the city. The Zone boundaries were marked, with Han Chung Road on the south, Chung Shan Road on the east, Shansi Road on the north (really a little north of Shansi Road), Sikong Road on the west (this road runs west of the roads a little west of Ginling College), a straight line across the hills to the corner of Shanghai Road and Han Chung Road. This formed the south-west boundary. This line cut through the seminary boys dormitory. But houses on the border lines were considered about as safe as those just inside the border. Practically the whole population of Nanking moved within this area. All houses were filled to overflowing. In the absence of any responsible person in charge at the B.T.T.S.,[1] I asked the pastor of the Ku I Loh Methodist Church to move into the Ladies' faculty residence, and take charge of the place there. His occupancy of that house assured us that it would be in good hands. There are about four thousand people housed on the campus of the B.T.T.S. In our own seminary, there are over 3,100 people. At both places of course hundreds of people are living in little mat-sheds erected on the campuses. The entire Refugee Zone is a city of mat-sheds. All public and private houses are filled to capacity.

With the coming of the Japanese soldiers we thought order would soon be restored, and peace would come, and people would be able to return to their homes and get back into normal life again. But the surprise of surprises came to us all. Robbery, looting, torture, murder, rape, burning—everything that can be imagined was carried out from the very beginning without any limit. Modern times have nothing to surpass it. Nanking has been almost a living hell. There has been nothing or no one safe. Soldiers have taken anything they wanted, destroyed what they did not want, raped women and girls openly and publicly by the scores and hundreds. Those who opposed them were bayoneted or shot on the spot. Women who have opposed being raped, have been bayoneted. Children who have interfered have also been bayoneted. One woman who was being

[1] Bible Teachers' Training School (for Women).

THE NIGHTMARE CONTINUES

raped on Fran's place—there have been about 150 people staying at his house—had her four or five months old baby near her, and it cried, so the soldier raping her smothered it to death. One refugee girl in the B.T.T.S. was raped seventeen times. Finally we got Japanese guards stationed at the gates of the larger compounds, but they often themselves go in and rape women. Every day and night brings forth repeated cases. These cases have occurred by the hundreds—they make a tale of horror almost indescribable.

But we are still living in hopes—hopes that a better day may soon come. But when—we cannot now see. The homes of many people have been burned, and shops and stores are still burning. Every day and night fires can be seen in the city. Nearly all of Taiping and Chung Hwa Roads have been burned out. Nearly all the important business and shopping districts have been burned. The Chiang Tang Chieh Church and the Y.M.C.A. have been burned to the ground. So the people cannot all go home even when they might be able to. Many of the villages outside the city have been burned. Shunhwachen has been burned, we hear, but not the Rural Church training center.

We have a big refugee problem on our hands now with this large number of people—perhaps 150,000 or more in this Refugee Area, and perhaps 60,000 in our Refugee camps. Many of whom have to be fed. Our food supplies are very short, and unless something can be done to get more suplies, famine conditions of a most serious nature face the people. Our International Committee has a supply of rice on hand for about three weeks yet—we do not know what we will do after that time. We are trying to buy rice from the Japanese (Chinese rice they have commandeered), but they are holding it apparently anticipating a long war, and keeping it for their own use. I am busy distributing the rice each day to the various centres. Riggs is supervising the coal and fuel supplies to the various rice kitchens, and others are doing other things—all together trying to carry on and help improve the conditions as much as possible. But our task is not an easy one. We are trusting in the Lord and doing our best at it. He can well see through it, we verily believe.

The servants of the B.T.T.S., three school servants and your own servant, have asked about the whereabouts of Miss Smith, because they are needing their wages. I told them I would try to get in touch with you, but that I would pay them regularly myself, so they need not have any fears—we can make these financial adjustments later. I am looking after the finances of the seminary group of course—including all the caretakers of the various houses, so finances are not our chief difficulty. I am glad to say that all of our servants have been most faithful and loyal and helpful in these trying times.

I am sending this letter by the British Embassy official who is going to Shanghai today. They will have a gunboat returning to Nanking immediately, so if you wish to write me a line, you can send it by the British Consulate there.

PS. It is needless to say that all of our houses have been thoroughly ransacked—Chinese and foreign alike. But the houses themselves have suffered very little damage. Our Married Students' quarters were pretty much wrecked by a bomb falling about fifty feet away just before the coming of the Japanese. Books and heavy furniture have not been molested much, but smaller valuables, warm clothing, foods, valuables, bedding, bicycles, automobiles, cows, horses, pigs, chickens—have been taken almost with a clean sweep. But the story is too long to continue—and too heartbreaking.

A chronology of cases of disorder by Japanese soldiers reported between January 1 and February 9 appears in Appendices B and C.

CHAPTER V

TERROR IN NORTH CHINA

THE FOREGOING PAGES *have dealt almost exclusively with the conduct of the Japanese Army during their occupation of Nanking on December 12-13, 1937, and after the occupation up to about February 9, 1938. This method of presentation has been followed because Nanking was the main objective of the Japanese Army, and because a proportionately large and international group of foreign residents remained there throughout and kept meticulous records of events.*

It should not be supposed, however, that the events at Nanking were by any means exceptional. Similar outrages against civilians have been reported from widely separated regions of China ever since the beginning of hostilities in North China in the mid-summer of 1937.

No attempt is made here to give an exhaustive account of happenings elsewhere. Such an undertaking would require a volume very much larger than the present one. Instead, and following the general method of presentation in the earlier chapters, eye-witness accounts from various centers, large and small, will form the bulk of this chapter.

Without exception, the writers of the subjoined accounts are foreigners with many years' experience in China, and, in some cases, in Japan as well. In each instance the letters in which they recorded their impressions were intended not for publication but for the information of an intimate circle of their friends. As such they form a straightforward picture composed of intimate details of the happenings around them. Withal, it will be noticed that fairness is implicit in their accounts and, indeed, that restraint is the keynote. The names of the writers are omitted only because many of them are still engaged in relief activities in the districts from which they write, and publication might prejudice their ability to continue.

On September 18, 1931, were fired at Mukden the first shots which resulted in the creation of "Manchukuo" and the domination of Manchuria by Japanese militarists. From 1932 to 1937, Japanese forces applied gradual pressure in North China, especially in the Peiping-Tientsin district. On July 7, 1937, what has come to be known as the "Marco Polo Bridge Incident" occurred on the outskirts of Peiping as the prelude to a large-scale Japanese drive in North China. Japanese troops poured into the Chinese Provinces of Hopei and Chahar daily, until by the end of November some 300,000 soldiers were on Chinese soil and, having driven the Chinese troops out of the greater part of these two provinces, were forcing their way into the neighboring provinces of Shansi and Shantung. Peiping and Tientsin were rapidly taken, by the Japanese forces, which then proceeded to capture Paoting, provincial capital of Hopei, some eighty miles south of Peiping.

The following letter from a neutral foreign observer describes events in Shansi from early September to mid-December:

Peiping, December 17, 1937.

Dear ———,

I left Paoting for Pingting, Shansi, on September 4 after quite a little bombing had been done in that city, but it was not occupied by the Japanese until some two weeks later. In Pingting I stayed with friends in the Brethren Mission and as a group it was decided we would stand by and await the Japanese occupation.

On October 23 our communications with Taiyuan, the capital of Shansi, were broken, and on the 25th bombing planes filled the air from five o'clock in the morning until five o'clock in the evening. No bombs were dropped in the city of Pingting as no Chinese soldiers had been stationed in the city. Some fell on the barracks less than two miles distant and many at the railroad station five miles away. That night many Chinese soldiers passed through the city, and the city police and officials fled to parts unknown. The next day, before daybreak (Thursday), we could hear the fighting, and by the next morning could see the tearing up of the ground and the smoke from the big guns. On Friday about four o'clock from my window I saw the planting of the Japanese flag on the city wall, and soon the troops poured through the gates. Since then we have been living under the rule of the Japanese. Our own compounds flew the American flag. The house in which I was living had a great American flag painted on the roof.

War is WAR, no matter what country is carrying it on, and I am glad that in reading *Gone with the Wind* during the summer I had some realization of what had taken place in my own country some seventy years ago. From 1,000 to 1,500 Chinese fleeing from their homes flocked into our compound. The first week of occupation by the conquering army will always be an indescribable nightmare. Many of our refugees were girls or young women, which the people were trying to hide. One instance will show how they were hunted down. In one home the mother was sick on the kang, and they hid their young daughter under a cupboard in a most cramped space. The soldiers looked everywhere for young women in the place and even came in several times during the night to see if some one had not come out of a hiding place. For two days and two nights the girl scarcely dared to breathe in this hole and was not in a position to eat, before they could get her out and to a Mission compound. Hundreds of women were hidden in nearby mines. One group of over two hundred was rescued by an American nurse after having been without food for over two days. Another group was betrayed and carried off. The Mission housed refugees in three compounds inside the city as well as in the hospital compound outside the gate. One compound was not Mission property so could not fly the American flag. One day two soldiers came over the wall and grabbed a couple of young girls and carried them back of a house. Mr. C. was sent for and fortunately arrived before they were injured. During the day one or another of the foreigners stayed in these compounds during those first frightful days. At night over seventy girls and young women slept in our house, and all other houses were equally full. You may guess we did not undress and did not sleep very soundly. . . .

After the main part of this army had passed on, Pingting was used as a base for supplies and sending soldiers north and south, east and west, so there has been a constant coming and going of troops. Those coming from the front would rest a day or so and loot and rape. The soldiers and their horses were quartered in the homes of the people, appropriating everything they wanted in them and using furniture, doors, everything of wood about them, to build their fires. I have been in homes in which nothing was left but the brick walls and dirt floors. The first lot that came in spent four days and went through books and everything written that they could find, gathering anything they could against everybody they could in the city. The shops as well as the homes were completely emptied of everything. If anything was left troops coming later picked it up. Anyone whose clothes had any resemblance to those of a soldier was killed on the spot without questions. One man I knew who happened to have grey inner trousers was thus cut down. Men were taken to serve them and if they did not understand immediately what was desired of them they were killed. So many tales one could tell. Yet this is WAR.

As they took possession of all food supplies, food was becoming more and more of a problem. Many of the refugees had neither food nor money. Several hundred of those in the Mission compound were being fed by the Chinese Committee organized under the Japanese. Those who had money were finding it increasingly impossible to find anything that could be bought. The soldiers had eaten or carried off the pigs, sheep and chickens, so meat had to be very limited in our diet. They also absorbed everything in the line of fresh fruit, but some vegetables could be obtained. Fortunately the Mission families had had a big yield of tomatoes in their garden. . . .

These things I am telling you out of the limited experiences of my own weeks in the midst of HELL. When one thinks of the great areas of this country of which this is a fair sample, it is too awful to contemplate. At no time did I feel in any personal danger. Mr. C. early established relations with the officers of the conquering army and we met some very fine Japanese men, some of them had studied in American institutions. The soldier's attitude depends upon what kind of a man he is, and some of them are bad and some of them are good. . . .

PAOTINGFU

Another letter, describing events in the Paoting district, follows:
Paoting, December 10, 1937.

By way of introduction for some who may see this let me explain that I have been keeping a diary that I head 'As It Happens' intended chiefly just to share with my family. Some matters that I have excluded from its pages I wish to record and comment upon here. . . .

Now let me mention a few concrete matters of which I have intimate knowledge. It is now eleven weeks since the change of regime in this area, so we are somewhat away from the heat and the confusion of the actual war zone,—no main theater of war within sixty miles of us for two months.

For about seven weeks of this period we had here but a small army of occupation, and little movement of troops to and fro,— probably less than two thousand Japanese here at any time. The body in control was the 'gendarmerie' here for maintenance of law and order. A fair amount of police order within the city walls was brought about within a month and has been maintained there since, so that for the most part the populace in the city feel as secure as in normal times. Yet the following incident happened but a few days ago and I am told that like occurrences are not infrequent: Three Japanese demanded entrance to the premises of a well-to-do resident. Caretakers were there but the owner away. He has held much of his wealth in the form of valuable antiques and Chinese works of art of different sorts. The Japanese helped themselves to all the more valuable objects they could find. . . .

The first of the week one of our staff went to a nearby village to see the officers of a local cooperative society that we have helped foster. Soldiers live in some of the private premises of that village. At night, if anybody locks doors and does not open at once when the soldiers come along they break the door in. The night before soldiers had made a house-to-house search over the whole village with flashlights for women. That day a villager had been clubbed to death for the offense of not producing any women for them. . . .

The common people around us ordinarily depend largely on leaves, grasses, and grain stalks for winter fuel,—affording little wood. But the Japanese search for wood everywhere, that they use in prodigal fashion for quick fires. As a result, loose wood now being exhausted, doors, window frames, furniture, farm tools, even the frames of houses that they are pulling down are rapidly being used for fuel. One of our refugee women was telling today with tears in her eyes of losing a weaving loom for fuel. 'It is my one means of livelihood,' she said. Just across the street from us is a yard that belongs to our native church. In it is one house built some thirty years ago semi-foreign style, with well carpentered panel doors. Day before yesterday two of these were wrenched off for fuel, and the others being strongly held by rusty screws, the soldiers just splintered out the panels from several of them. Yesterday we took off the remaining ones and stored them in our compound. Yesterday several of the soldiers scaled a back wall into a little side court off our main compound and before we knew it had sawed down a tree of five-inch diameter. When my American colleague accosted them just after the deed was done, they did seem a bit shame-faced. . . .

I haven't arranged items in any order of climax, but have tried to give a bit of index to the aftermath of war in this particular zone. Just now in an interruption I have heard another fully authenticated story of three men, tenants in a yard not far to the south of us, who have taken a heavy beating for letting their women get out of reach,—one left with teeth knocked out, another with such a bruised leg that he can not bear weight upon it.

Are such happenings as I have mentioned the necessary aftermath of any war? Maybe War would make it worse! Aren't we told that the present expedition was just to settle 'a local North China incident'? No war has been declared. But, at any rate, now that trouble is on, 'there must be a fundamental settlement of the China question.' And 'this concerns just the two countries.' It is for no third party to intervene. Any settlement must be on the basis of an understanding for 'cessation of all anti-Japanese propaganda and effort' and of 'full cooperation against Communism.' And what excellent methods are used among the populace to get such fundamental understanding! Is psychology—either theoretical or practical—completely banned from army circles?

I haven't the least wish to condemn a whole people with any such words as I have here tapped out. Nor even would I, by any means, condemn all who are in the army. I could list for you a goodly number of instances of fine sympathy and human goodness on the part of individual soldiers and officers, that have come within the range of our knowledge or observation right here. And more than one have told me that they would prefer not to be at this, but 'we are under orders.' There you have it. They are caught in the meshes of a system, and carried along hardly half aware of what it is all about and where it is taking them. God, pity these men! and pity this old world that still does not cure itself of the terrible malady of the war system! Are we Christians so helpless as we have seemed to be hitherto to bring some remedy for war madness? How much are we actually undertaking to do?

These words are intended particularly for some of my closer friends and relatives. I trust that they will not fan the flames of hatred on the part of any of you, but that they will equip you a bit for further thinking, and for giving testimony where ungrounded propaganda is spreading falsehood. . . .

A GENERAL SURVEY

The following extracts have been taken from a confidential report headed "As It Looked in North China, February 1938" sent by a well-known American missionary to his colleagues at Shanghai:

Conditions throughout the countryside, south and west of both Peking and Tientsin, are best described as those of 'unprecedented lawlessness and anarchy,' as Mr. Pennell, editor of the *Peking & Tientsin Times,* put it on Feb. 16. Most of what he said in an article in the January Number of *Oriental Affairs* under the title of 'Anarchy in North China' remains true. There is, however, a slight difference in that in some sections this 'anarchy' is becoming somewhat organized, if such an Irish way of expressing the truth may be permitted. That is, with all the former organs of government removed except from the immediate vicinity of the railway lines and a few garrisoned county-seats and market towns, something has begun to come in to fill the vacuum. This something seems to be of three varieties: (1) local bands of bandits looking out only for themselves; (2) more socially minded groups, such as the revivified 'Red Spears' who are particularly active in parts of Shantung but are also found in southern Hopei; and (3) mobile units of Chinese troops, with or without organic connection with the increasingly famous 'Eighth Route Army,' the so-called Communist element in the national defense. All three types are united in their wholehearted hatred of the Japanese; the first type, of ordinary bandits, are hunted down and exterminated when possible by both the other two; and the third type gives promise of absorbing or consolidating the second.

In the meantime all three add immeasurably to the difficulties of the occupying forces. There are stories galore of their exploits, many of which have a good chance of being preserved as parts of a new collection to rival the fables of 'The Three Kingdoms.' They have certainly put the fear of something into the hearts of the Japanese all along the Peking-Hankow line. At Paoting Japanese soldiers no longer venture far from their barracks after dark—thereby removing one of the greatest causes of anxiety from the hearts of most civilian families. The garrison at T—— is reported to have been wiped out three times by sudden raids.

The tragic side of this is the retribution which is so frequently meted out to people living near the scene of Japanese reverses. After one of the attacks on the garrison at T—— a large number of civilians were reported to have been burned to death with kerosene or gasoline taken from the local stores of one of the foreign agencies. . . .

The Father Superior of a group working in Shantung reached Peking only a few days before I came away. According to Dr. P. he reported atrocities repeatedly occurring in their vicinity of the same type that became so familiar here when news began to come out of Nanking. The ill treatment of women was not confined to houses and courtyards but was extended to the open streets, and on one occasion a civil officer had beaten one of the foreign priests. In Shansi the Japanese advance in November stopped short a little distance south of Pingyao, some thirty miles beyond Taiku. The hills on both sides of the plain have been held either by semi-independent mobile units or by forces directly connected with the Eighth Route Army, and frequent raids have kept the invaders in a chronic state of jitters, but have led to as frequent reprisals on the helpless villages who have remained within the area of activity.

One of the ways in which an enormous amount of useless destruction of property has occurred is through the ignorance on the part of the Japanese of the use of coal. Many of them apparently know how to burn nothing but wood, even when large stocks of coal are available. They have therefore ransacked villages for fuel with a total disregard to its source. Doors, windowframes, posts, rafters, tables, benches, wooden farm implements, timbers of all sorts, have been carried away or yanked out of the buildings and used for cooking and heating. In one of the gates at Paoting an enormous bonfire was kept going day and night in an extravagantly wasteful manner, and anything wooden that could be laid hands upon was considered legitimate fuel.

One of the worst stories which I heard was brought in only the day before I left Peking. A band from the Eighth Route Army had come down to the railway track not so very many miles from Paoting and requisitioned labor from the near-by villages to tear up the track. They did the job so well that for six days there was no through train between Shihchiachuang and Peking. (This we know from reports in the French newspaper—the *Peking Chronicle,* the official foreign-language organ of the new Government, had denied any such thing only two days before.) But in due time the railway was repaired and Japanese troops came on the scene in some force. They visited one of the villages and at first appeared bent on no particular errand. Shortly afterwards however they rounded up two hundred of the men of the town, took them out and shot them. When a long enough time had elapsed so that the terror-stricken people had for the most part returned to their homes, they suddenly appeared again and this time seized sixty of the huskiest young men of the village. It became known that these men were to be burned, but in some way during the confusion of making the preparations for the burning, somebody was able to set them loose and they all escaped. Two old men were thereupon seized and substituted for the younger men. As the narrator put it, people of that region have since determined that henceforth they will refuse to assist in any guerilla warfare efforts on the part of Chinese troops. 'It is better to be shot by our own people for disobedience than to suffer in this way at the hands of the invaders.' This raises an important question which I shall refer to a little later. The man who brought this story went on to say that as he came north on the train to Peking he saw a village very near the railway in flames, with a cordon of troops surrounding it, who were actually shooting people as fast as they tried to escape from their burning homes. After very careful questioning, one of my closest Chinese friends, a man with whom I have been intimately associated during the past seven years, was convinced that the village must have been the one in which his own wife's parents and other relatives have always lived. A member of the staff of the ——— Embassy received a report just after this that all the villages near the railway track for a long distance in that region had been burned. . . .

CHAPTER VI

CITIES OF DREAD

SHANGHAI AND THE Yangtze Delta were brought into the orbit of hostilities when on August 9 a Japanese officer and a seaman acting as his chauffeur were killed when driving a car in the vicinity of the Chinese military airport at Hungjao, on the western outskirts of Shanghai.

The story of the war in the Yangtze region is one of heroic failure on the part of the Chinese troops in their attempt to dislodge the Japanese from their positions in the International Settlement in August, and an even more heroic resistance to the increasing Japanese pressure of men and metal from ships, land and air until, after a series of repeated withdrawals, the Chinese Army found itself outflanked again and again and so was forced finally to retire from Shanghai on November 14.

After having occupied the main cities and lines of communication embracing the Shanghai-Soochow-Hangchow area, Japanese troops succeeded, as has already been related, in breaching the walls of the national capital itself on December 13.

The subjoined accounts tell of the death and destruction left in the wake of the Japanese Army's swift advance through what is normally one of China's most peaceful and most densely populated districts.

According to a careful estimate made by a foreign observer who had visited these regions on several occasions, both before and after the Japanese occupation, at least 300,000 Chinese civilians have lost their lives as a result of the Sino-Japanese hostilities in the Yangtze Delta. A considerable proportion of these people were slaughtered in cold blood. This observer spoke of old men and young boys having been forced by the Japanese soldiers to carry burdens far beyond *their strength and, when they fell down from sheer exhaustion, having been bayoneted and flung into a ditch by the roadside. Nor were the dead spared from ill-treatment. At many points along the line of march, he stated, Chinese graves were opened up and the coffins burned. It was the considered opinion of this observer that in its advance upon Nanking the Japanese Army had adopted a policy of deliberate terrorism.*

The following graphic account was telegraphed to London by a British correspondent who visited Sungkiang, a walled city thirty miles south of Shanghai, on January 14:

Sungkiang, which was the original headquarters of General Gordon's "Ever Victorious Army," and a thriving city on the Shanghai-Hangchow Railway, presented a scene of indescribable desolation and destruction. Acres of houses have been laid waste as a result of aerial bombing, and there is hardly a building standing which has not been gutted by fire. Smouldering ruins and deserted streets presented an eerie spectacle, the only living creatures being dogs unnaturally fattened by feasting on corpses. In the whole of Sungkiang, which should contain a densely packed population of approximately 100,000, I saw only five Chinese, who were old men, hiding in a French Mission compound in tears. They were short of food and begged to be taken back to Shanghai.

The condition of Sungkiang is typical of the state of affairs throughout this densely populated delta between Shanghai and Nanking, and testifies to what may have been one of the greatest mass migrations of population in history. No one is able to answer the question of what has happened to the hundreds of thousands, or rather millions, of Chinese who have literally disappeared from this area. The whole thirty-mile route between Shanghai and Sungkiang is like a desert, with rice crops ungathered and left rotting in the fields as far as I could see. The traveller passes a continuous vista of blackened ruins and burnt-out farms guarded over by gruesomely fattened dogs.

Considerable bodies of Japanese troops returning to Shanghai were passed on the road. They represented a strange appearance, being loaded up with piles of loot from the countryside. In many cases rickshas containing trunks and suitcases were hitched behind cavalry horses and Japanese soldiers were riding donkeys, cows, and even buffaloes, collected from the countryside. Live pigs were tied to artillery limbers, and chickens were carried which had been taken from farms miles from the route that had been visited by foraging parties. At one point on the road was a huge concentration of Japanese supply wagons, and several batteries of field artillery. My attention was caught by thousands of cases of Japanese beer which had been consumed by the Japanese troops.

SOOCHOW

Soochow, known as the "Venice of China," is a picturesque city on the Shanghai-Nanking railway line fifty miles west of Shanghai, with which it is also connected by several new motor roads. It is known to thousands of tourists who make only brief visits to China. Its normal population is about 350,000. Following the retreat of the Chinese troops from the Shanghai area, the city fell, practically undefended, to Japanese forces on November 19, 1937.

The following account of events in Soochow, written by an American, appeared in a supplement of the China Weekly Review, *Shanghai, March 19, 1938, entitled "Destruction in China."*

SOOCHOW NIGHTMARE
An Almost Incredible Experience in the Shadow of Bursting Shells, Looting, and Assaults on Women

(*The writer, a resident of China for more than thirty years and whose name, for obvious reasons, is withheld, reports the following eye-witness account of terrorism and atrocities by the Japanese army.*)

It was our helplessness, the impotency of 350,000 human beings—the aged, young and feeble of the beautiful, tradition-steeped city of Soochow—in the path of Barbarians at War which struck us with nauseating force that day in the second week of November when Japanese bombers first began releasing high explosives upon the city proper.

It was a frightening thing to see; a horrible, maddening thing under which to dwell—tons of explosives hurtling down from the skies, exploding in a cascade of bits of human flesh, dirt, stone and mortar. Both night and day death rained upon the city from the circling, droning Japanese planes.

At the early stages of the bombings, the majority of the fear-crazed residents of Soochow sought sanctuary in dugouts. Finally, air raids became so incessant that we debated whether to remain in the dugouts or return to our work and take our chances on missing death. We decided on work.

On November 9, handbills were dropped from planes, warning Soochow that, after three days had elapsed, the entire city would be even more intensively bombed. Could that be possible? We were already living in a veritable inferno. This warning: that the grand old city of Soochow would be practically destroyed, brought before me a tragedy too realistically terrible to put into words. I cannot pass on to you the feelings that came over me as I saw hundreds of thousands of men, women and children leaving their homes, carrying with them their pitifully small belongings.

By this time, however, boats, rickshas and other vehicles could not be obtained at any price, and most of the refugees had to flee by foot. My companions and I had previously secured two boats from Chinese soldiers, and it fell to my lot on the night of November 12 to tow these boats by motor launch to Kwangfu with our first contingent of refugees. I immediately returned to Soochow for another load where Chinese soldiers commandeered the two boats, but left me the motor launch. I turned the launch over to my companion and he, with other friends, started off again for Kwangfu.

It was now too late to enter the city gate so, with a friend, I spent the night in a deserted hospital. It was the night of the big air raid. And only God and the people left in the doomed city of Soochow knew, or ever will know, the horrors of that night. The most dreadful nightmare could not compare with it. The entire city and its environs were lighted with flares dropped from planes. And then death started on its speedy flight from the skies. No human being could have counted the number of bombs released upon this defenceless city. One might as well have tried to count the drops of rain falling on a like number of square miles in twelve hours' time. My friend lay flat upon the floor. At times, I got under the bed. Strangely enough, I felt safer there.

At daybreak, we arose and went into the city. The death and destruction we witnessed defies all description. We felt nauseated, sick. The only cheering sight we saw was a Chinese pastor leading a thousand refugees towards Kwangfu. What a picture! Behind him trailed small children, old men and women, the lame and those disabled by bombs and shells—I thought of the Good Shepherd leading His flock. In two days, five thousand refugees from Soochow had been removed to Kwangfu.

I, myself, left for Kwangfu and it was not until November 21 that I returned. My companion and I had to drive carefully to avoid running over bodies of the dead lining the roads and scattered over the fields. When we arrived, looting on the part of uniformed Japanese soldiers was proceeding in lively fashion. Mission property, as yet, had not been molested. From that time until December 11, we went into Soochow nearly every day. We saw that every bank and shop and every residence had been forced open. Japanese soldiers were passing in and out of them, like ants loaded down with bales of silk, eiderdown quilts, shop goods and household effects of every description.

On one of our trips, however, we found that mission property had been looted thoroughly. The front, back and side doors of one particular building had been forced open. The doors to the school buildings and residences had been smashed in, apparently with axes and butts of guns. All rooms had been entered and all trunks and boxes broken into. Such things for which they had no use were scattered in wanton confusion over the floors. In my home, the dishes had evidently been thrown upon the floor with great force. In my friend's home, we saw his son's violin on the floor, broken beyond repair.

During one of my visits to Soochow, I went into the Administration Building of Yates Academy. I came upon a group of soldiers before they were aware of my approach, catching them in the act of breaking open the school safe. One soldier was striking the safe door with a pick-axe. While a group was attempting to smash the safe, others were rifling desks in the offices of the principal and the dean. When I went to the end of the hall to call an interpreter, they left, taking their tools. In another hour's work, however, they would have had the safe open.

Leaving the compound, we heard music in the church. We entered and found a Japanese army officer playing the piano, while several of his soldiers were rifling desks in the conference room of the auditorium. I rebuked him for allowing his soldiers to loot the church. He saluted and left immediately.

The next morning we returned and found that the soldiers had finally forced open the safe and robbed it of approximately $400. Amusingly enough, however, is that the looters threw on the floor about $300 in pay envelopes, thinking they were useless letters. We found, too, that safes in several other mission compounds, as well as the strong boxes in banks and shops had been smashed and their contents carted away. The "fine discipline" of the Japanese army apparently was no more than a myth.

Actually, blame for wholesale looting in Soochow cannot be placed upon individual soldiers, but rather upon the Japanese army as a whole. More loot was taken than could have been carried away by individuals and, furthermore, we saw much of this loot being loaded on army trucks. One truck, loaded with expensive blackwood Chinese furniture, stood in front of the Japanese army headquarters.

The dead bodies we saw on the streets in Soochow on our first visit there after Japanese occupation, lay there for ten days or more. On our later trips to the city, we observed that the street dogs were noticeably fatter. Equally ghastly were the buildings, damages amounting to more than a million dollars.

All that I have recounted is terrible, but the worst remains to be told—the violation of women of all classes. None can possibly estimate the number of women ravaged by the lust-mad Japanese army. Personally, I know of enough cases to make me believe all the reports that I have heard. After all, what difference does it make in such wholesale assaults whether the number is 9,500 or 9,600? One morning in Kwangfu, I met a young student of Soochow University who told me, with tears in his eyes, of the attack upon his beautiful sister. Again, I saw great numbers of village men sitting by the roadside, trembling—a band of armed Japanese soldiers had driven them from their homes keeping behind their wives and daughters.

That night I was asked to stay at the home of a Chinese in order to help protect his daughters and other young girls who had come there for safety. It was well that I did, for that night at about eleven o'clock I was awakened by a flashlight shining through my door's transom. Someone whispered 'Japanese are here.' I secured my flashlight and rushed into the adjoining room. There I saw three Japanese soldiers flashing their lights into the faces of the ten or twelve young girls sleeping on the floor. My presence surprised them and, at the sound of my angry tones, the marauders hurried down the stairs. The Chinese father stood by my side during these very tense moments.

I have told this story, because I cannot live with it hidden in my heart. And, should anyone believe that the Japanese army is in this country to make life better and happier for the Chinese, then let him travel over the area between Shanghai and Nanking, a distance of some 200 miles, and witness the unbelievable desolation and destruction. This area, six months ago, was the most densely populated portion of the earth's surface, and the most prosperous section of China.

Today the traveller will see only cities bombed and pillaged; towns and villages reduced to shambles; farms desolated, and only an old man or woman here and there digging in the once "good earth." The livestock has been either killed or stolen, and every sort of destruction that a brutal army, equipped with all the modern implements of war, can inflict has been done here.

And where are these people now who have been driven from their homes?

Countless numbers have been killed; others have been maimed for life; yet others are huddled in refugee camps, or hiding in mountain caves, afraid to return to their desolate farms, their empty shops and ruined businesses. Those who would dare return are not permitted to do so by the war-mad Japanese army.

It is shameful, indeed, in the face of all this, that the Japanese who control communication lines, are proclaiming to the world that they are inviting Chinese back to their ancestral homes to live in peace and plenty.

WUHU

Wuhu with an approximate normal population of 140,000, is a thriving Yangtze River port 58 miles south-west of Nanking and about 263 miles south-west of Shanghai. For many years it has been an important mission center. The town fell to the Japanese forces on December 10, 1937, three days before the fall of Nanking. The following extracts from the letters of a foreign missionary in Wuhu describe events during and following the occupation up to December 30, 1937:

Wuhu, December 17, 1937

Since the war has come to our Wuhu area you, no doubt, have been thinking of us as we have of you. I will send a brief statement of some of the things that have been happening here. A summary of events beginning December 5 will give you an idea of the conditions under which we are living during these days of crisis. On Sunday, the 5th, while we were in church service the hum of planes was heard overhead, which was coming to be a commonplace occurrence, when all at once there was a succession of terrific bomb blasts. The audience rose to their feet as one man. We suggested the windows be opened and that there was no cause for alarm. We then continued the service for about ten minutes when an even larger series of terrific blasts were heard. On going to the front of the building, we saw one of the Jardine boats in flames and great clouds of smoke rising from what seemed to be the railway district. After watching the planes for a few minutes until they seemed to be going away, I asked for the car to be brought to the gate, but found that our chauffeur could not be located, so I drove the car myself taking one of our staff with me. We were at the bund within half an hour after the planes left, and started sending wounded to the hospital. The casualties of this bombing were especially severe as the people were not prepared for it. Dead and dying were all around. I went onto the British gunboat and found considerable shrapnel had struck the ship and slightly wounded Commander Barlow. Their crew were busy pulling people out of the water, and the ship's doctor was already giving first aid to some of the cases. The British tugboat was going alongside the burning "Tuckwo" helping in the removal of those on the ship. The B. & S.[1] ship "Tatung" had just come alongside their hulk preparatory to taking the hulk away. It was also struck but not set afire and immediately proceeded to the opposite bank of the river. During that afternoon and night we received one hundred at the hospital for treatment. More than eighty of them needed to be admitted and the staff performed thirty operations during Sunday afternoon and night, besides the treatments given in the admitting rooms.

The days since December 5 have been rather hectic and strenuous for us. We were bombed three days in succession, and all roads leading from the city were crowded from dawn to dark with the city's population seeking places of safety. Pathetic sights passed our gates. Families carrying what bedding they could for the enforced exile among the hills and fields, babies on parents backs or in baskets on the carrying poles, all with drawn anxious faces made up the procession....

The Japanese troops have occupied the city in increasing numbers since the 10, establishing artillery batteries at the railway bund and just below the B. & S. bund. They have been ruthless enough in their treatment of the few soldiers who had remained, not knowing of their arrival. Civilians who have not complied with their every demand have been treated in like manner. Any moving junks or sampans attempting to cross the river have been riddled by machine guns. One such boat with three occupants drifted ashore below the hospital and they were brought in for treatment. One of the men had ten bullet wounds....

December 30, 1937

Every day of the past month has been full of exciting, difficult, and at times dangerous experiences, but so far not one of the more than 1,400 people on our hospital hill who entrusted themselves to our protection and care has been lost. Every day has been a challenge to our ingenuity, patience and loyalty to protect them against the soldiers who frequently demanded admission at the gates or climbed

[1] Butterfield and Swire.

over the compound wall, and to provide shelter, food, sanitation, and control for this large number who are living in a place with housing facilities for only four hundred.

During the first week of occupation, the ruthless treatment and slaughter of civilians and the wanton looting and destruction of the homes of the city far exceeded anything ever seen during my twenty years' experience in China. The Chinese soldiers did not enter or disturb any foreign property in Wuhu. However, the Japanese have entered and looted nearly every piece of foreign property in the city. The two or three places that have escaped were those where some of us Americans stayed by to keep them out.

Probably conditions in Wuhu have been less severe than in most places because there was little fighting here. The soldiers seemed to especially seek Chinese women for violation and the saving of these women became one of our major activities over a period of several days. I did not hesitate to go out into the city with one or both of our cars to pick up women wherever I learned they were in hiding. On some days I made as many as four trips bringing back carloads of younger women and girls. If our cars had never rendered any other service, they have been worth far more than their cost during these few weeks and I hope some way may be found to express special thanks to the friends in Albion and Ann Arbour, Michigan, who gave these cars to me. Without them, it would have been utterly impossible to have saved these women or to have brought in provisions to keep the institution going.

I have kept in constant touch with the Japanese military authorities and the Japanese Consul who recently arrived. They give strong assurances for the protection of American lives and property and I have been using all the strength of my influence to get them to control their soldiers in their violence against Chinese civilians. They assure me their soldiers are forbidden now to molest the Chinese or to force them to serve them, and most of the officers desire to prevent these offences. In spite of these promises, it is still not safe for any Chinese man and much less for a woman to go on the street. Two of our hospital servants whom I sent out two days ago on a trial trip were robbed and made to carry loads. I immediately sent a letter of protest to the commanding officer and received his apology with the return of the money, but those who are not protected in this American compound have absolutely no redress.

An American flag was torn down from our hospital junk on Dec. 13. I immediately went to the junk, fished the flag out of the river with a bamboo pole, and then took it, still wet, to the Japanese commanding officer. I also reported this incident and several others to our American authorities in Shanghai and since then have had representatives call to make apologies from the Japanese Navy, the Japanese Army, and the Consul. Since the bombing of the U.S.S. "Panay," they seem very anxious to make amends to Americans. Several of the wounded Americans and Chinese from the U.S.S. "Panay" were brought to this hospital for treatment.

Conditions have been such that it was not safe for our hospital men to go out and bury the dead that were accumulating in the hospital morgue. Our supply of lumber for making coffins also ran out. Finally, it was necessary to dig one large grave on the hospital compound in which we buried twenty bodies. . . .

HANGCHOW

Hangchow, "the Lakeside City," which was reportedly visited by Marco Polo, is one of the beauty spots of China and has a normal population of about 800,000. It was occupied on December 24, 1937, at 8 a.m., by Japanese forces, the vanguards of which consisted of the Fujii unit. Hangchow was practically undefended. The account following consists of extracts from the letter of a foreigner who stayed in Hangchow throughout the occupation, the letter being in the form of a report to friends abroad:

Hangchow, January 27, 1938

Dear ———,

Early in November there was a Japanese landing in Hangchow Bay which seems to have been practically unopposed and this resulted in all Chinese troops in the Shanghai district being left with no defences to the south and a general retreat began which did not really stop till after Nanking was captured in December. Day by day we heard of this town and that being captured and it seemed to all that if the Japanese wished to capture Hangchow it was very likely that they could. . . .

On Sunday, Dec. 19, rumors began to fly thick and fast—the Chinese army staging a very complete and successful retreat beyond the river engaged the Japanese forces in great strength, by wireless! and nobody knew where we were really until one day all the bridges on all the roads round Hangchow were blown up, the Governor and the Mayor departed and all officials. On Dec. 22 in the afternoon after due warning given our Big Bridge and our most efficient Electric Power Plant were blown up with a tremendous explosion, our waterworks machinery was dismantled or destroyed, during the night the Police left and we wakened on Dec. 23 to a deserted town in every way defenseless. Then alas, the dregs of the populace covered itself with infamy for a large number of the rice shops were badly looted, a number of schools were stripped of all their furniture and one could meet a stream of people for all the world like a stream of ants in the neighborhood of any of these schools and of the well equipped Chekiang Government University, with students' desks, chairs, stools, beautiful laboratory tables, anything made of wood, all intent on heaping up a store of fuel 'while there was time' and no authority to prevent them.

The city fathers had arranged a force of six hundred "specials," members of our little back street fire brigades, but they only looked on, helpless to stop the looting, and then on Dec. 24 the Japanese came!

Our planning to save Hangchow seemed to have been successful, except for the looting by the populace, for now we felt we would be in the hands of a modern equipped and disciplined army and, though occupied, all, we thought, would be well.

The Japanese evidently knew that there was no likelihood of resistance for on December 24 the troops just straggled in, in no sort of military order and with no sort of military precautions, and starting Dec. 24, they just strolled in, in twos and threes, rifles slung on their backs with no scouting, no preparation, no nothing, till our streets were gradually filled with little bodies of Japanese infantry, very tired, wandering aimlessly about looking for food!

As soon as possible we got in touch with the first regimental Commander to arrive and told him we hoped to cooperate with him, etc. etc. The city fathers got orders about rice and food which were rendered more difficult to comply with after the looting of the day before which continued into the next morning. While we talked to him we heard of two people shot by the soldiers, one because, not understanding Japanese, nor the writing of a Japanese soldier, he turned away rather quickly, the other because he tried to run away—a Japanese soldier who spoke Chinese is reported to have said "This man tried to run away" and shot him!

However, we hoped these were isolated occurrences and we went to bed that night feeling that the long strain was over, that our determination to hold on to the Hosiptal work exposing our foreign women and our many Chinese girl nurses to all the possible perils of warfare had been justified and that now we only had to readjust ourselves to the Japanese regime and carry on in peace and safety. . . . I was personally reminded of Christmas Eve 1926 in an old home in another part of China, when we were similarly "occupied" by 'the Northern Expeditionary Army,' and expected for ourselves and our children and the Christian community generally, a time of great trial. Then our anxiety was turned to peace when the Southern Commander turned out to be a Christian and we were freed from all fear, but *now* when we expected peace we were very sadly disappointed.

Our hopes were still high as Christmas morning dawned. We had our Hospital Holy Communion Service at 8 a.m., English Celebration for the A.P.C. patient and another Britisher at 9, there was a 7 o'clock celebration in the city church and we assembled for our regular 10 o'clock matins and celebration with quite a good congregation considering how almost everybody who could had fled.

But on my way home from Church I began to doubt, the street was full of straggling troops, not in any sort of order, mostly with rifles slung and not at all prepossessing in appearance (infantry after ten days or so on the march are like that!), and as I turned round into the main street for the Hospital I saw a fierce-looking fellow with his entrenching tool neatly going through the shutters of a little shop and taking the whole front down and at the other side of the road there were members evidently of the same ration party going from shop to shop right along the street and then stories began to run through the streets of looting and pillaging all over the town so that our refuges, which some of us thought the day before might not after all be needed, began to fill up with frightened women and their numerous small children. Throughout the day, too, airplanes droned overhead continually and heavy artillery fire was kept up for hours as the Japanese harassed the Chinese on the other side of the river.

Then began for me a few days of very real "shepherding." It began on Dec. 26. We had been a little disturbed on Christmas night by heavy knocking at various parts of the Hospital—all round the compound there are old entrances that have gradually become disused and more or less blocked up—it was the 'less' in several of these that gave us pause and on the morning of Dec. 26 Dr. Sturton and I went on a tour of inspection all round to see what further strengthening was needed. When we were just about half-way round getting to the north-east corner of the Hospital we met several women who asked our help—we told them to go to the Wayland School some ten minutes' walk away where there was a Red Cross refuge. They said they wouldn't be taken in and as they continued in that strain I said I would go with them. Then began a calling and shouting to friends and relatives and children and requests to me to wait a while for this one and that and for one from another house till I was like the Pied Piper with women and children for my following as I led them through the streets, through a lot of halted Japanese soldiers to the Wayland gate outside which there was a crowd of about a hundred people clamoring to get in.

I got in touch with the Chinese in charge of the door and asked him to open for this group of about forty people I had gathered up and the others who were waiting. "I can't," he said, "we are all full up." "Nonsense," said I, "the women must get in—call Mr. Clayton, please." He was the American missionary in charge of this refuge. When he came along he said they had already about eight hundred inside but as they had planned to take a thousand he would let this group in—the Chinese helpers said if we were not careful men and all would rush in so I spoke to the people and told them the refuges were only for women and children and they would all be admitted "but you men must go out of the way to the other side of the street!" which they did very willingly and just about ninety women and children were admitted. That was my first "shepherding" but for a few days after that I made two or three trips each day to the various refuges taking along ten or twenty women and children full of terror at the things that had happened to them or that they had heard of and feared. Generally these little bands collected at the Hospital. From the morning of the 24th we had to have the outside gate locked and a foreigner in charge. The first couple of days I was on guard a good deal helped by Dr. Phyllis Haddow and Miss Garnett, but later Miss Garnett became 'Horatius' and for about a fortnight she kept the gate all day, deciding who could and who could not come into the Hospital. On the 26th when I was going to the front gate at about 9 o'clock in the morning I found a thick stream of people pouring into the Hospital for refuge. I had the gate shut at once and we gradually sorted them all out, some had to go straight out, men mostly, women we gathered into the out-patient preaching place near the front gate and then I led off those who wished to go to the refuges. We were a sorry sight; mostly poor women with several children in arms and toddling along holding their mothers' skirts and biggish girls with nondescript bundles of bedding, clothes, household utensils, etc. etc. Straggling along and being halted every few minutes to keep them together making our way slowly through streets with a large number of Japanese soldiers, not generally actively interfering in any way but putting terror into the hearts of these women as they just looked at them!

Each morning found more and more frightened women thronging to get into the refuges and from one thousand inmates the two biggest ones rose through fifteen hundred and two thousand to over twenty-five hundred. What a sight they made inside! Camped out, for example in the Union Girls' School, the crush at the door, the gradual sorting out inside, the putting into places already crowded beyond possibility of lying down, more and even more little groups of mothers and their big daughters and all the little ones, till in a dormitory building of three stories, bedrooms, corridors, porches, verandahs, landings on the staircases were all crowded tight, and in a huge cement-floored gymnasium behind hundreds were packed in the space they took up as they sat—there they sat all day, there they were fed and there they slept—a sight to turn anybody against war and its sufferings and yet these were the fortunate ones! How they were fed, mostly one meal a day and that cooked with great difficulty! How they were kept in a reasonably sanitary condition only the devotion of the Chinese helpers and the adaptability and reasonableness of the patient Chinese women made possible, but there they were in such conditions, not for our originally planned four days, but as I write it is the thirty-fifth day and it is not yet safe for the women to go to their homes.

We soon got settled into a routine life. Dr. Sturton was freed from all duties in hospital so that he was available for helping in every conceivable sort of outside duty with the Hospital car or ambulance. Here is the sort of thing he did: Dec. 27, 9 a.m. Report from the Roman Catholic Convent on the City Hill that Japanese soldiers are actually inside and frightening the women refugees. "Can the C.M.S. Hospital help?" Off goes Dr. Sturton, with a Japanese officer who was visiting the Hospital, in the ambulance and the soldiers are evicted, the Convent abandoned and the women taken by ambulance to the Roman Hospital a couple of miles away. 1:45 p.m. same day. Phone from Roman Catholic Church: "Can C.M.S. Hospital do anything?" (We had a phone kept on when the city system was stopped, joining us as center to the R.C. Church, the College and our Branch Hospital at Sung Mok Dzang.) Dr. Sturton again with a Dr. Tanaka of the Japanese forces goes off at once, finds the Roman Bishop Deymien beaten in the face by a drunken soldier who was continuing to threaten the Bishop with his fixed bayonet till Dr. Tanaka drove him out; and so off in the ambulance for a load of wood to the other end of the city, hoping the Japanese ration parties will not "commandeer" it at sight, or for rice for one of the refuges, or for coal for the Hospital or to take the guards round to our six posts, etc., etc. Any of us at any time were sent off for that sort of job but especially Dr. Sturton, while Dr. Haddow got her very capable hands on the regular washing of the hospital, and Mrs. Curtis became extra busy with the many babies who came from the refuge camps to our maternity department to be born and Miss Garnett kept the gate, and as for the rest, the student nurses had all their regular lectures and the whole work of the Hospital, doctoring, nursing, etc. etc., wounded soldiers, civilians, babies, went on day and night in its ordered course. . . .

I mentioned "fire" a little while ago—anybody who knows the position of the Hospital right in the heart of the city with a fairly wide street on the south side and typical old-fashioned Chinese streets on the other three sides, and into the middle of our south side a block of old dilapidated Chinese houses running, and on our west, south and north sides in places rather miserable old lath and plaster buildings, and inside a large proportion of our buildings just made to burn up quickly, will realize how dreadful a thing fire seems to us. On Dec. 26 as I was finishing shaving I happened to look west and as it seemed between me and the Sturtons' house on the extreme west of the Hospital a huge column of black smoke was rising and as I looked it burst into flames and the hospital bell began to sound the fire alarm. I shouted to my companion, threw on an overcoat and ran out to find all the hospital workers rushing to the west of the hospital. As I got towards the front gate I saw the fire was outside the Hospital so I went into the street west and saw there was a good twenty-foot wall on the other side of the street and the fire was well inside that. Then back to mingle with the Hospital people beginning to remove patients from the Hospital block in the west, north of the Sturtons' house and to tell them it was not immediately necessary, then I got up to the third story of the foreign sisters' house a little more to the north and thence one could see the fire clearly and observe first that it was burning away from us and that we could not be in danger unless it moved through a couple of walls and came back twenty or thirty yards but second that if it did so the sisters' house would be in extreme danger as one can almost shake hands across the street west of them from some ramshackle back buildings of ours to some more wooden structures on the other side of the street—with a west wind and a fire there we would be in serious danger. However, that Sunday we were able to get back to breakfast in a short time but our 8 o'clock celebration had to be cut out!

From that time there have been many fierce fires in the city but that was the nearest to us though twice at least there were fires near enough to force us to go and see actually where they were and on yet another occasion the night staff nurse who is also due to call me if necessary called me to look at a fire that seemed to her too near to be pleasant. Miss Woods' household half a mile north of us was got up twice and out on to the lawn for that fire which was in her street. . . .

It was quite a treat to go to see Miss Woods (and it became routine on my part after a day or two), to visit her from (refugee) centers and Mr. Taylor's of which more anon, each morning at about nine o'clock. I became milkman for that community early on when the milkman dare not take his milk into the streets. You might meet me any day with four pint bottles divided between the side pockets of my overcoat and a half pint in my breast pocket—one of our blessings was that we have had fresh milk (in the Hospital!) on every day but one all through—and see the order and enjoyment of life there—a kindergarten school, a primary school, a middle school and a Bible School for women all running by timetable all the time —it was an oasis of order in a very disorderly world. Miss Woods got in touch with the soldiers billeted all round her centers and had no trouble but quite a deal of help from the men. On New Year's day outside a billet between the Church and Miss Woods' house I saw on the wall in chalk "Dear Mr. Bishop, A Happy New Year to you." There was a notice signed by me on the Church door—hence this greeting! This was quite a happy spot in the unhappy city, tho' even then from nearby Miss Woods and her helpers were continually rescuing women and girls from the prevalent danger. For since the occupation besides looting all over the city—I doubt if one shop or house anywhere was left unmolested and in addition in many places horses were stabled in shops and houses so that our beautiful Hangchow soon became a filthy, battered, obscene place—there were reports from all directions of women being ill-treated. The frightened groups ouside the refuges each day told their own tale and we have in hospital among other damaged women, two women with broken backs, one of them has both legs broken in addition, both injured as they jumped from upstairs windows to escape pursuing soldiers. The city became a city of dread where robbery, wounding, murder, rape and burning all added their share to the cumulative fear and only in our foreign compounds and in the refuges was there any sort of security.

The authorities and especially the Military Police did their best to help *us foreigners* but for the city at large there was *no help*.

Chinese were left there at the mercy of any soldiers whose dispositions led them into evil doing and when we had opportunity to protest the authorities professed to find it hard to believe such stories and consistently treated them as of little importance.

The Military Police were excellent but all too few in number: one of the first days just as it was getting dusk the hospital business manager Mr. Dzen rushed in as I was having a late tea after some scurrying round and besought me to go to his house in the next street and help him, as two soldiers were there looting. Not very happily I went and just as we got to the corner of the Hospital to turn down into the other street we saw a military policeman standing beside his bicycle giving directions to some soldiers; so Mr. Dzen rushed at him and began to write down in Chinese an appeal for help and he came right away with us. We (he rather!) caught one man in the house using a long sword bayonet and taking his name etc. he marched him off to the police headquarters. . . .

When we bring these misdoings to the notice of the Japanese authorities we are sometimes expected to be comforted by the words "you should see Shanghai or Nanking or Kashing!"

What it is all to mean to our Church work we can't tell. The Chinese and Japanese armies have been all over our three country parishes in the Hangchow District Church Council and we shudder at what may have happened having seen the happenings in Hangchow. So far the other three District Church Councils across the river have not been invaded and we pray that they may be saved from this horror, but everywhere terror stalks through the land and the stories we discounted to our Chinese friends before the Japanese occupation we can only now sorrowfully confess do not fully portray the horrors actually experienced.

In Hangchow there was a wonderful opportunity for the Japanese Imperial Army to show how a disciplined army can take possession of an undefended town but alas the opportunity was not taken. There was no defense, not a Chinese soldier left in the town, and the Japanese evidently knew in advance that this was so but instead of the soldiers being kept in order and the townsfolk being encouraged to keep the life of the town going, now five weeks after the occupation one can hardly walk anywhere in the city without seeing looting openly carried on by soldiers without any evident attempt by the authorities to interfere, and even now hardly anywhere is a woman safe.

As far as we foreigners are personally concerned we have not much complaint to make; only, as far as I know, three assaults, and these not very serious, have been made on foreigners, strangely enough one on each of the three nationalities represented, Bishop Deymien of the French Mission, Dr. McMullen of the American and Mr. George Moule, British, retired from the Chinese Customs Service and living in Hangchow (the son of a former Bishop of our Church here). The assault on Mr. Moule at his age, well over seventy, might very easily have been very serious. Our properties have been kept reasonably safe, tho' actually on our properties several of us have been threatened with rifle or pistol by intruding soldiers. This safety however only obtained where foreigners have actually been in residence; elsewhere no national flags, consular notices, church notices, military police notices availed to stop continued intrusion and looting. Even places which the Military Police wished to help us to protect had to be abandoned in the end and were visited continually and the contents gradually disappeared. . . .

WUSIH

Wusih, aptly nicknamed by the Chinese as 'Little Shanghai,' is an industrial center with a peacetime population of about 900,000. It is about 105 miles due West of Shanghai, to which it is connected by several motor-roads and by the Shanghai-Nanking Railway. The following account of happenings at Wusih was printed in the special "Destruction in China" supplement of the China Weekly Review, *Shanghai, March 19, 1938:*

DIARY OF AN AMERICAN DOCTOR IN CHINA
Medical Man's Recordings are Indictment of Brutalities by Japanese in Warfare.

No more graphic account has been related of the last days of Wusih before the war-mad hordes of Japanese military descended upon the city, than this odyssey of an American doctor who left Shanghai October 14 for the doomed city, his motorcar loaded with clothes, food and medical supplies in order that he might alleviate the sufferings of the wounded and the hungry. His trip was a perilous one, taking the road on which two days previously three cars, carrying the British flag, were machine-gunned by Japanese planes.

His description of scenes witnessed a few miles before he reached Wusih is a damning indictment of the brutalities of Japanese warfare. The bombing of coal barges on the canal near the road, the shooting of helpless farmers in the field, the descending of planes upon innocent groups of peasants, machine-gunning them and following those who lived to run and firing upon them again.

His story of hardships, the daily caring for sick and wounded under the constant threat of death from the rain of Japanese bombs, is written in diary form. The following is his personal record:

October 16. A Chinese was brought to the hospital today, his intestines so badly torn by machine-gun bullets and the subsequent loss of blood made his case hopeless. When the Japanese planes approached, he ran for cover in a mulberry grove. The planes followed and machine-gunned him. At the same time, three other farmers were killed and four wounded. There were no Chinese soldiers within miles. Why, or for what purpose could these Japanese attack poor country people who are perfectly harmless?

October 17. This morning I went on ward rounds with the hospital staff. The building is crowded with wounded soldiers and a few civilians. Pitiful were those soldiers with legs and arms amputated and those who are so badly wounded. It is just a matter of time until they pass away. Certainly, it is a horrible thing. There were three women, each of whom had a leg amputated, after being injured during the severe bombing at the Wusih railroad station October 6.

We found the staff had built three huge bombing shelters below ground on hospital property for those who wanted to take cover during an air raid. The power plant which furnishes Wusih with electricity was disabled by bombs recently, so we have no juice for X-rays during the day, but a temporary plant gives us power at night. Then we are able to get radio news from Shanghai, provided there are no air alarms which means 'all lights out.'

October 18. Early today, just as we were starting on ward rounds, the siren sounded and we knew the Japanese planes were Wusih-bound. We kept on with our ward round, although we all had a gentleman's agreement that it is quite proper to seek shelter in the dugouts. Soon we could hear the heavy drone of planes. Then came the terrifying sound of the ships power-diving which always precedes the bomb explosion. I didn't know what this American hospital was in for and, although a colleague and myself continued our work, I couldn't honestly say that I was taking much interest in the cases. However, we both had previously decided that we couldn't run out of the wards and seek protection while helpless patients had to remain in bed. Soon the sound of bomb explosions reached our ears and we guessed that it was the railway station which had been hit. There are no defense works here and not a shot was fired at the ships which dropped four bombs in all. Shortly, a railroad guard was brought to us, the side of his head smashed by shrapnel. His condition was so critical he had no chance of living. Several others were killed and wounded in this bombing.

October 25. No bombings have yet occurred within the city walls and I don't believe any will. I wouldn't be anywhere else for a million dollars and I hope I can be of some use here. The hospital itself is plainly marked with American flags and in Chinese characters which are the same in Japanese.

October 30. No air raid today, but several alarms were sounded, warning of planes passing in the distance. Still no electricity and no prospects of getting any.

October 31. A direct hit on a Chinese hotel today completely destroyed it. The policeman on duty near there escaped shrapnel which splattered all around him. The terrific noise made him deaf.

Bombs destroyed the clock tower and pitted the road with craters. The station had two direct hits and the freight godown was burned. We crossed the tracks and saw where a bomb had landed directly in front of the Washington Hotel and the Brothers' Hospital yesterday.

November 1. Local Chinese newspapers promise electricity soon. Hope it's true. As I write, a Japanese plane is circling overhead. Wish this war was over. Made tentative arrangements to resume my language classes with a former teacher in the Soochow Language School who is now in Wusih.

November 3. Two Japanese seaplanes arrived this morning and bombed for about twenty minutes, directing their missiles at empty trains. Later, when I was amputating some fingers, or what remained of them, on a soldier who had been struck by shrapnel, another plane came over. Fortunately for the operation, no bombs were dropped near us. We hear that the telegraph wires to Shanghai are cut and that the Japanese are crossing Soochow Creek while the Chinese continue to fall back.

November 4. Japanese planes raided us this morning during Chapel. They dropped bombs across the city wall, the closest to us as yet. They quite startled us as the plane motors were quieter than usual. Probably a new-type bomber. A train was hit and several people killed.

November 5. The lights came on today for the first time in three weeks. I found myself in much disfavour with the crowd when I blew a fuse out in attempting to plug in the radio. However, after the electrician fixed it, we failed to get the raido news because a boxing match was being broadcast.

November 10. This has been our worst day by far for bombings. Conservatively, 160 of them were dropped, causing heavy damage and several fires. The areas bombed were the mountain at Wei Sei, outside the city, the mill districts and the area beyond the

West Water Gate. At 11.30 p.m., I was hounded out of bed by heavy explosions. From the window I could see a Verey light descending slowly, lighting up the whole city. Apparently the light revealed nothing worth-while, and the plane passed on. I learned that many wounded soldiers were killed in the bombing today when a military hospital was hit at Wei Sei, besides countless deaths among civilians in the mill districts. Civilians brought to our hospital were terribly mangled. A man had his left ear torn to shreds, his left biceps muscles almost severed, a long penetrating wound in his left thigh, his right foot torn almost in half (amputation will be necessary) and his genitals badly mutilated. He had a dozen other smaller wounds. Goodness knows where we will put patients if this bombing around here continues.

November 11. Planes bombed Wusih for an hour this morning deliberately picking their targets. I was in the operating room at the time and the sterilizer was making so much noise the explosions didn't bother me so much. In the afternoon bombing, the missiles came much closer, landing within a few hundred yards from the hospital. The house trembled again and again, and furniture danced a jig. I felt the urgent need for a cigarette.

We immediately went to the hospital and found that several pieces of shrapnel had hit it. The nurses seemed quite calm, but one or two of the doctors were jittery. We learned that the big normal school had been hit. Shortly, four horribly wounded civilians were brought in with legs and arms dangling grotesquely and all requiring amputations. I worked with a colleague in removing a man's leg at the knee and extracting a piece of shrapnel from his thigh. He also had a shrapnel wound in his buttocks where a piece had entered fracturing his coccyx and perforating his intestine. Now I am waiting for supper, and other operations are posted for tonight and tomorrow.

We heard a touching story today. When the dugout here was struck October 28 and all its forty occupants killed, there was a young child in there who was so terrified that no one could stop it from screaming. Believing planes would discover the hiding-place because of the noise, the mother was told to take the child out. She refused. The father finally carried the tot to a position behind a tree trunk. A few minutes later, a bomb hit the flimsy dugout and all inside were killed.

November 12. Today was a nightmare. A Chinese soldier, wearing a steel helmet, was sitting in the window when the Japanese bombers came over. He immediately ducked inside, but a few seconds later the bombs started hurtling down, falling on all sides of us. I'll admit my reaction was self-preservation. I crouched down, noticing at the same time that the room was clear of nurses. I was scared to death and sick with fear. I was ashamed of myself for being so. The bombs continued to fall with ear-deafening explosions. I knew that some of them had fallen just outside and I was relieved not to be hit. Almost immediately, they began bringing in people injured in the bombardment. The first man brought in had died of fright. Other cases of severe shock came, but I knew they had no chance to live. Another man with bad chest injuries was hopeless. A father called us to aid his daughter whose thighs were fractured, and his son, with one eye shot out. An old man came carrying his feeble wife upon his back. She was lacerated with shrapnel. In they came in droves, victims of Japan's attack upon civilians. Some are of the opinion that the planes overshot their marks, but I believe the bombing was intentional. They were flying low and could not fail to distinguish the very large freshly-painted American flags on all the roofs besides the flags flying over the two compounds. The damage to the compound was terrific. Walls were smashed, telephone poles riddled and the wires down. Projectiles had gone through neighbouring houses and debris was scattered all over the place. The exodus from Wusih is beginning. I can hear our neighbors nailing up doors and windows and moving out of the city as fast as they can. The Chinese staff is deserting en masse. The hospital chief hasn't said yet what he intends to do about this desertion except that it will be impossible to keep the hospital open and that our next step will be to get the remaining patients moved out. Although I might not enjoy it, I will stay to the last ditch if some of our staff members reconsider and decide to try and keep the hospital open. I reckon I'm a sissy, but I'm still scared.

November 13. None of the doctors appeared for duty today and we learned that some of them had left the city during the night by means of a military truck. The nurses are frantic to get away, but there are no buses available, all are being used at the front. The hospital chief feels terribly about turning the patients out of the hospital. The worst part of it is, he has no way to move them. None of those remaining here are willing to help. The chief feels he may be criticized, but he has no other alternative. The place is lonely. Tonight there is only the gateman, one or two coolies, and a few nurses who are staying only for one or two days because they are unable to find transportation. The cooks, laundrymen, firemen, mechanics, carpenter, operating room coolie, druggists, laboratory men and all the doctors have gone. It would be impossible to care for these patients were we to keep them. Thankfully, some of the patients are well enough to leave by themselves and by tomorrow I think we shall have only about a half-dozen to care for.

Bombing here probably hasn't been so bad as it has at Soochow and other places because there haven't been any troop concentrations here. However, the bombing has been unexpected and cruel for that reason and the fact that Japanese broke their precedent and bombed within the city walls.

Word came through tonight that we can get our wounded soldiers moved to a military hospital. That's a relief. But it also means that it won't be long before the battle line is here.

November 14. I started the motor of the old car this morning to see if it would run. It was all right. I tied an American flag to its roof. We have decided to leave before daybreak tomorrow.

November 15. We left Wusih at 5:30 a.m. driving through the wreckage at West Gate. This area was swarming with soldiers, preparing to take cover for the day. Rickshas, carts and hordes of persons were streaming through the gate, fleeing from the city. The air was tense. You felt that panic was on the verge of breaking out.

Every town we passed through we saw great crowds waiting for buses; however, the further we got away from Wusih the more normal things appeared. Shortly after 11 p.m. we reached Nanking where great military activity was taking place. My one thought is, however, to get back to Shanghai.

November 19. We left Nanking yesterday and today we are anchored off Chinkiang. We leave tomorrow for Kowan where we will have to take small launches to go inland by canals. This move is to avoid the river booms.

November 21. Back in Shanghai again! And now, in the quiet of my home with my war-time moustache shaven off, I have much to be thankful for. But I cannot forget the misery we left behind us. We have been gone for slightly more than a month, but in that month I have seen enough to make me hate war forever. The misery and the suffering it brings to the innocent civilians is indescribable. . . .

CHAPTER VII

DEATH FROM THE AIR

RARELY IN HISTORY *can civilians have been wiped out by aerial bombs in the wholesale fashion witnessed during the Japanese invasion of China. There is virtually no important city in China, save in the remoter provinces, which has not been visited by raiding Japanese bombers since the first attack on August 15 at Nanking by Japanese planes which flew across the sea from Formosa. Japanese aerial activity in North China in July and early August 1937 was insignificant in comparison to attacks from August 15 on throughout China. The widespread character of the Japanese aerial attacks can be judged by the following Domei*[1] *report from Tokyo, printed in the* Shanghai Evening Post and Mercury, *an American-owned English-language daily, of November 3, 1937:*

TOKYO, Nov. 2—(Domei)—Eight-hundred and fifty naval planes took part in attacks on Chinese positions on the Shanghai front and the hinterland between Oct. 25 and 27, a spokesman of the Admiralty revealed today.

These aircraft, he added, dropped in all 2,526 bombs, weighing 164 tons. The consequent Chinese losses, the spokesman asserted, were high. . . .

The Osaka Mainichi, *an English-language paper, in its edition of October 15 stated that Japanese planes had bombed more than sixty places of "military importance" in the two months which had elapsed since the initial bombing of Nanking on August 15. The cities which had been bombed (to Oct. 13), as listed in the Mainichi, were as follows:*

SHANTUNG PROVINCE

Hanchuang, Tsaochuang, Yenchow, and Tsining.

[1] Domei is the official Japanese news agency.

KIANGSU PROVINCE

Nanking (including Pukow), Shanghai, Kuyung, Wusih, Kiangyin, Soochow, Kunshan, Kiating, Taitsang, Sungkiang, Suchow, Yangchow, Nantsung, Haichow, Lienyun, Huaiyin, and Nanhsiang.

CHEKIANG PROVINCE

Hangchow, Ningpo, Haining, Kienkiao, Kashing, Chuki, Kinhua, Chuhsien, and Shaohing.

FUKEAN PROVINCE

Amoy, Lungki, and Kienow.

KUANGTUNG PROVINCE

Canton, Sheklung, Fumoon, Waiyeung, Yingtak, Kuking, Lokchong, Kityang, Chaoan, Swatow, and Whampoa.

ANHUI PROVINCE

Wuhu, Kuangteh, Anking, Chuhsien, Pengpu, and Shuhsien.

KIANGSI PROVINCE

Nanchang, Shangjao, Yukiang, Tsingkiang, and Kiukiang.

HUPEI PROVINCE

Hankow (including Wuchang and Hanyang), and Siaokan.

HUNAN PROVINCE

Chuchow.

Commenting editorially on this report in the October 30, 1937, issue of the China Weekly Review, *Shanghai, Mr. J. B. Powell, editor of the* Review *and himself an intrepid eye-witness observer of Japanese military activities, stated:*

This list of towns, few of which have any possible military significance, probably has been doubled by this time, particularly when the dozens of villages and hamlets in the Shanghai area which have felt Japanese frightfulness, are included in the list. On Sunday afternoon (Oct. 24) the writer observed about two dozen planes, ten of them twin-motored monoplanes carrying six bombs each, which were engaged in bombing the farm villages, most of them one-family-and-relatives hamlets, located in the farming and gardening area stretching northward from Soochow Creek. A foreigner who had observed the bombing in the morning stated that 18 planes had been engaged from daylight to noon and that approximately 200 bombs had been dropped, most of them of the largest variety, weighing in excess of 200 pounds. The number of bombs dropped in this area in the afternoon probably exceeded 150, making a total of 350 in a territory that could easily be observed by the naked eye. The Japanese aviators staged a veritable field day of destruction, going through most of the antics they would perform had it been a public exhibition for entertainment purposes. Squadrons of three or four planes would power-dive from high altitudes dropping missiles of great weight and explosive character upon Chinese farm-houses made of bamboo and mud-plaster with tile roofs, the whole structure probably not costing more than the equivalent of $40 or $50 in American currency. Fortunately most of the occupants of these farm-houses had evacuated, or had become wise in the art of dodging. But despite the precautions one observed a few wounded civilians, usually elderly women, making their way or being carried toward the Settlement. At one place on Soochow Creek some villagers were observed burying five civilians in one grave, a crater created by a Japanese bomb.

Some idea of the strength and power of the Japanese bombs was provided by the size of the craters produced by bombs dropped at the corner of Pearce and Rubicon roads. Here the bombing was of some military significance because the Chinese have a sand-bag outpost on the bank of the creek and in addition they have constructed a trench system in the vicinity. A half-dozen bombs dropped here left craters ranging from twelve to eighteen feet across and probably six or eight feet deep. But the sand-bag redoubts on the corner were missed entirely while the trenches that caved in were quickly repaired. None was injured on this occasion. The villages along this creek paid a heavy toll in earlier bombings, but now most of the villages are deserted, except for a few elderly persons. But many farmers and gardeners still hang on and continue to work in their fields, even when bombs are dropping within a few hundred yards. The foreign and Chinese populations of Shanghai can thank these farmers and gardeners for hanging on because they have kept this city from starving. The long strings of peasants with baskets of vegetables, observed along the outlying roads, tell the real story of the hardihood of the Chinese sons and daughters of earth.

The headlines over the reports of death and destruction published in the local papers tell their own stories of the tragedies which have become commonplace. For example, JAPANESE BOMB SUNGKIANG, KILL TWO HUNDRED, WOUND FOUR HUNDRED—FORTY KILLED IN ONE DUGOUT SHELTER.

The Chinese withdrawal from the Chapei sector on Wednesday afternoon provided the Japanese airmen with another opportunity for slaughtering noncombatants. The armed Chinese forces withdrew across the Soochow Creek bridges at Jessfield under cover of darkness, hence were not molested by the Japanese airmen. Thousands of Chinese civilians, chiefly women and children, packed the roads and single-track railway bridge crossing Soochow Creek on the following morning. The opportunity for slaughter was too tempting to resist apparently for a Japanese pilot repeatedly flew low over the bridges and machine-gunned the crowds of terrorized people. On one occasion he left a dozen dead and an equal number of wounded, including several women and children, lying on the bridge. Similar scenes were enacted on most of the outlying roads.

Against the charge of indiscriminate slaughter of civilians, Japanese military and diplomatic spokesmen have repeatedly reiterated that the objectives of Japanese aircraft are exclusively military. They have also asserted that press reports of their aerial activities are "much exaggerated" because of "mendacious Chinese propaganda." Can such claims be accepted? Is Japanese bombing of civilians a mere accident, something incidental to military operations?

It would be impossible to give here a comprehensive answer to the above question but the subjoined newspaper and eyewitness accounts will enable the reader to form his own opinion.

AROUND SHANGHAI

Shanghai and its environs soon felt the brunt of Japanese aerial attacks. On August 28, 1937, Japanese airplanes bombed the South Station, Shanghai, which at the time was crowded with refugees. The British-owned and edited North-China Daily News, *an English-*

language daily published in Shanghai, reported the tragedy in its issue of August 29, 1937, as follows:

TWO HUNDRED REFUGEES KILLED IN RAID ON SOUTH STATION

Japanese Bombers Litter Nantao Streets with Death and Destruction

Chinese Deny any Soldiers in Area

Shanghai's civilian casualties mounted considerably yesterday when Japanese bombers raided densely populated Nantao, littering the South Railway Station area with death and destruction. According to a conservative estimate, well over two hundred persons, most of whom were refugees, were killed or wounded. The list is by no means complete, as the over-worked hospital authorities in the Chinese city, French Concession and the Settlement were checking the number of cases last night.

The death-dealing mission was composed of twelve Japanese planes at about 1:45 p.m. Leisurely circling over the South Station sector, the raiders dropped no less than eight bombs, most of which exploded.

Crowded with over one thousand refugees, most of whom were women and children, the station was worst hit. Other places where missiles exploded were Kuo Ho Road (Native Goods Road), two blocks to the north of the station; San Kuan Tang Street, and Loh Ka Pang area.

Altogether four bombs landed around the station. As the airplanes finally left the scene, dense smoke shot up high into the sky, while on the platforms and tracks were scattered charred and badly mutilated bodies.

The first bomb exploded a short distance from the station, wrecking a water tower close to the tracks. Many fell, killed by shrapnel outright or pinned down by debris. As wounded persons ran for shelter, a second one descended, tearing down an overhead bridge and damaging a section of tracks. Blood and wreckage strewed the immediate vicinity. At the same time, terror reigned in streets close by as additional missiles exploded one after another.

The South Railway Station has been the gathering place for refugees seeking transportation to the interior ever since the outbreak of hostilities two weeks ago. Many of those killed yesterday were known to have been patiently waiting for accommodation in Hangchow-bound trains during the past two or three days.

The wall close to the booking office of the station was smeared with blood, as mutilated bodies piled up at its foot. A large number of refugees were crowding the office to secure tickets and a bigger crowd was on the platforms when the raiders appeared overhead.

Death overtook many of the refugees who attempted to push their way into the administration building, but failed owing to congestion and the narrow passage. The building itself was only slightly damaged, window panes being shattered to pieces. . . .

Scores of students stationed in the Ta Tung College played heroic parts as they rushed to the station, doing the rescue work. They were practically the first on the scene, removing debris and helping the injured on to lorries which arrived shortly after.

Many of the wounded were rushed to hospitals in the city, but a large number came to the Settlement. The Lester Chinese Hospital reported about 100 cases, mostly women and children. The operating rooms were kept busy until evening.

When a representative of the *North-China Daily News* visited the Lester Chinese Hospital in the afternoon, extra beds were seen being placed in wards. A group of the wounded were brought to the hospital by Chinese ambulances. One baby, badly wounded, was picked up from the side of its dead mother. At least two children, each aged about thirteen, lying in the hospital, lost their parents.

The hospital reported last night that two women, two men, a boy and a girl succumbed to wounds. Several deaths were also reported by Paulun Hospital.

Terrified refugees, many of whom bore tags, were transported into the Settlement by lorries supplied by charity organizations. The South Station was barricaded for repairs and other work.

The bombardment of Nantao evoked the bitterest denunciation

from the Chinese military spokesman at the daily press conference yesterday afteroon.

Japanese allegation that the station was bombed 'because it was used for the transportation of Chinese units from the south' was most emphatically refuted. The spokesman stated that not a single soldier could be found anywhere in Nantao yesterday or recently.

Nantao is a densely populated city and entirely devoid of Chinese troops or military positions, he said. It was pointless for the Japanese to justify their attack by alleged intentions to 'harass Chinese military positions.'

The spokesman was at a loss to understand the wanton destruction of Chinese civilian lives. He said it was perhaps aimed at terrorizing the Chinese populace, or else as a retaliation for the loss of Japanese lives in Hongkew during the hostilities. He emphasized that no warning of the raid had been given by the Japanese.

A foreign correspondent at the press conference also confirmed that there was not a Chinese soldier in Nantao when he toured many streets in the city only recently.

Questioned as to the problem of evacuating Nantao citizens, the spokesman said it was most difficult in view of the railway lines having been constantly disrupted by Japanese aerial bombardment. Passengers were sometimes harassed by machine-gun attacks and bombing by Japanese planes.

Rubicon Village is less than an hour's drive from the heart of the Shanghai International Settlement. The little town was bombed several times, a typical account being the following from the North-China Daily News *of October 8, 1937:*

OVER 15 KILLED IN AIR RAID ON RUBICON VILLAGE

Seventeen Chinese, including a number of children, were killed in Wednesday morning's air raid by Japanese bombing planes on a Chinese village situated about a quarter of a mile from the Rubicon Inn on Rubicon Road. Chinese and foreign circles yesterday were unable to account for the raid, as it is reported that no Chinese soldiers are to be found in the village. . . .

According to the villagers the raid started at about 10 o'clock in the morning, when nine Japanese bombers suddenly appeared and dropped a number of bombs; the planes, it is alleged, then returned, to dive low and spray the village with a hail of machine-gun bullets.

Between twenty and thirty villagers were injured in this, the first raid. Those killed comprised the mother and wife of one villager, the two young daughters of another, the baby son of a third, and two as yet unidentified Chinese. . . .

In almost every case, the bombing of civilians has been followed by machine-gunning from the bombing planes or from accompanying fighting planes. Many of such attacks were, for the most part, witnessed by thousands of Shanghai residents. The Shanghai English-language foreign newspapers at the time were filled with protests from foreign eye-witnesses. The unending repetition of the attacks brought severe condemnation by Admiral Harry E. Yarnell, Commander-in-Chief of the U.S. Asiatic Fleet, who stayed in Shanghai throughout the hostilities there. Admiral Yarnell's statement was reported by the North-China Daily News *of November 13, 1937, as follows:*

CONDEMNATION OF BOMBING BY ADMIRAL YARNELL

"I have been grieved by the sight of so much destruction in and around Shanghai during the present hostilities and I wonder when mankind will realize the proper uses of aviation," said Admiral H. E. Yarnell, Commander-in-Chief of the U.S. Asiatic Fleet, when he and his officers were the guests yesterday of the Royal Air Force Association of Shanghai at the Weekly luncheon in "The Dome." There were rules for warfare as much as for any other activity, he said, and it was distressing to see the wanton destruction of property and lives of noncombatants by the belligerents and to realize the helpless plight of noncombatants here in Shanghai. . . .

"Rules of warfare," he went on, "must be observed and indiscriminate bombing and shelling should be studiously avoided." . . .

No useful purpose was fulfilled by wanton destruction of the property of noncombatants, he concluded, and it was time that the nations realized that aviation had far more uses than for the wholesale destruction its operation had affected.

Sungkiang is a peaceful city of about 100,000 *clustered around age-old canals and waterways, and is typical of the countless medium-sized centers which have been bombed. A semi-industrial center, it is thirty miles south-west of Shanghai and a station on the Shanghai-Hangchow railway line.* On September 9, 1937, *the* North-China Daily News, Shanghai, *described the bombing of a refugee train at Sungkiang in the following news report:*

300 CIVILIANS KILLED IN RAID ON SUNGKIANG

Japanese Planes Destroy Crowded Train

Scenes of Horror

Fleeing Local Refugees Meet Sudden Death

Yet another catastrophe overtook Shanghai refugees yesterday, when Japanese airplanes bombed a Kashing-bound train, killing three hundred persons, mostly women and children, and wounding an even larger number.

The raid was carried out at Sungkiang, first important station west of Shanghai on the Shanghai-Hangchow Railway, shortly after noon. Leisurely circling over the coaches, the bombers rained death on hundreds of refugees.

It was ascertained that five coaches were completely destroyed without a single soldier among the casualties. . . .

The time of the bombing was 12:20 p.m. when the train had just reached the platform waiting for the right of way to proceed to Hangchow.

How many Japanese airplanes took part in this raid on Chinese civilians was not specified in the reports, but it was known that they dropped scores of bombs at the station, wrecking, in addition to the five coaches, the over-head bridge, and the water-tower. . . .

Reports from railway authorities and Sungkiang officials depicted ghastly scenes at the railway station after the bombardment, with the place littered with blasted pieces of human bodies and blood-soaked debris.

The police and railway officials there were still busy in the afternoon removing the wounded to hospitals, of which there are not many in Sungkiang, while emergency burying corps were being sent for to take care of those killed.

Mr. O. K. Yui, Mayor of Greater Shanghai, who received the information of the bombing, bitterly denounced the "latest instance of Japan's complete disregard of human feelings by slaughtering Chinese civilians far behind the battle front."

"It was an undeniable fact that the train which was subjected to the most inhuman bombardment at Sungkiang was carrying refugees away from the war zone," he said. "The attack," he said, "was deliberate, and absolutely inexcusable, since the train was heading for Kashing and could not by any stretch of the imagination be considered to be carrying reinforcements to Shanghai."

The foregoing typical accounts of attacks on villages and comparatively smaller towns, by no means complete or comprehensive, have been given in some detail as they are perhaps less dramatic, although in toto far more ruthless and devastating, than simultaneous attacks on such large cities as Nanking, Canton, and Hankow which figured prominently in the world Press. The raids on Nanking continued from August 15, 1937, to the actual occupation of the capital on December 13, 1937. On December 18, 1937, the Reuter news agency reported from Tokyo that: "The Imperial Headquarters issued a communiqué today stating that the Japanese Naval Air Force visited Nanking more than 50 times and dropped more than 160 tons of bombs on Chinese troop concentrations and military establishments there from the outbreak of hostilities to the fall of the city. The communiqué also said the total number of airplanes which raided Nanking exceeded 800."

A summary covering a period of about one week consisting almost exclusively of extracts from Reuter reports from Nanking was published in the China Weekly Review, *Shanghai, of October 2, 1937. This summary follows, in part:*

JAPANESE REPEATEDLY BOMB NANKING DESPITE PROTESTS OF THE U.S.A. BRITAIN AND FRANCE

Ignoring the protests of Great Britain, the United States and France, twenty-nine Japanese planes visited Nanking during the early hours of Sept. 25 and subjected the capital to heavy bombing. South City, the most thickly-populated section of Nanking, received the particular attention of the raiders. . . .

The head-office buildings of the Central News Agency were completely destroyed and five of its staff members were seriously wounded during the second raid. Despite the disaster, the Central News Agency quickly adjusted itself to the losses and is now carrying on as usual. Altogether three bombs landed on the buildings which were situated at Tuchiakou, only a block from the famous Banking Circle. The region is thickly inhabited and is bereft of any establishments of military importance. The destruction of the news agency, which is a cultural institution, is generally believed to have been deliberately designed and executed to ruin the largest news gathering and distribution agency in China. . . .

The civilian casualties resulting from the air raid on Nanking, Sept. 25, amounted to six hundred persons killed and wounded. About five hundred bombs were dropped by the raiders, which made a rapid succession of five attacks on the capital city between 9:30 a.m. and 4:30 p.m. The Central Hospital and the National Health Administration which are situated on the same compound were the targets of two Japanese raids in the afternoon. Fifteen bombs exploded in the compound, though none of them scored a direct hit. One of the craters caused by the bomb explosions was twenty feet deep and forty-five feet in diameter. The dormitory occupied by the doctors collapsed from the force of the explosion. The hospital kitchen was wrecked and the operating room slightly damaged.

The bombing of the hospital, according to Central News, could not have been done by mistake, as a huge red cross emblem and four large Chinese characters equivalent to the words 'Central Hospital' were painted on the roof.

The auditorium of the National Health Administration, which has been cooperating with the League of Nations on health matters, was badly damaged. The adjoining institute for the training of health officers—an institution partially supported by Rockefeller funds —also suffered serious damages. Two Chinese servants were killed.

Among the victims of the Japanese bombardments were the Metropolitan Electric Plant and Waterworks, the Central Broadcasting Station at Kiangtungmen, the Municipal Health Station at Ssupailou, the Cantonese Hospital at Chungshan Road, and the offices of the Havas News Agency, Transocean News Agency and United Press Agency.

Bombs of 250 kilograms in weight were used in the attack on the new residential district, one making a huge crater on Chungshan Road, Nanking's main thoroughfare, at the corner of Shansi Road. Two missiles fell on a small hill at the corner of Ninghsia Road, badly shaking nearby residences, breaking window-glass and causing electric bulbs to drop from their sockets.

Bombs were also apparently aimed at the Ministry of the Interior and the Garrison Headquarters in the South City, but they missed their mark, and instead, destroyed a pawnshop. Seven residences, behind the Bank of China were also destroyed, but the occupants escaped injury, all having taken refuge in dugouts. The Telegraph Office also came in for attention, but the building was not hit, although several missiles dropped near it. . . .

A bomb was dropped inside the compound of the French Consulate on Hohui Street during the rain on Nanking by Japanese aircraft on Sept. 25. During the raid on Sept. 27, five bombs were dropped within two hundred meters from a French gunboat stationed at Sancharho, Hsiakwan.

Two raids previous to those above described were carried out by Japanese airmen on Sept. 22. An armada of over fifty planes participated in the attack, which lasted from 10:35 a.m. until noon; fifteen machines took part in the second raid, which was very brief.

An average of two or three bombs were dropped over three hundred different places, including the South City, and the new residential district, where the American, Italian, and German Embassies are located and where the residences of practically the entire local foreign population are situated. . . .[1]

After only an hour's respite, ten Japanese planes staged a second raid. They came from the north-east and, when they reached a point above Pukow, circled round in single file, and, power diving, dropped bombs one after the other, aiming at the Tientsin-Pukow Railway. Then they zoomed up and disappeared towards the north-east. According to officials of the French Consulate, four bombs, weighing five hundred lbs. each, landed during the raids on Sept. 25 within a hundred yards all around the Consulate. This was the closest shave any Embassy or Consulate has had so far. . . .

Canton is the Shanghai of South China. At the apex of the populous Pearl River Delta in the southern province of Kwangtung, Canton has a peacetime population of from 1,000,000 to 1,500,000. On September 23, 1937, the city was the target of a furious air attack, the North-China Daily News *of September 25, reporting the raid in the following Reuter[2] report:*

[1] The Reuter report cited here by the *Review* also included these details: "Although the exact number of casualties has not yet been determined, it is believed that more than one hundred refugees were killed when bombs landed on a camp at Hsiakwan, Nanking's waterfront, during the second raid. . . .

"The site of the refugee camp at Hsiakwan presented a gruesome spectacle when visited after the raids, with the twisted remains of the victims scattered over a wide area. The mat-sheds housing the thousands of refugees, set alight by the bombs, were still burning. The smoke of the flames, rising in huge columns into the sky, was visible for miles round. . . ."

[2] This *Reuter* report was criticized as being exaggerated and untrue by Japanese spoksmen, following which Reuter categorically denied the Japanese allegation, and issued another report giving further corroborative details.

THOUSANDS DIE IN CANTON
WHEN PLANES ATTACK

Scenes of Horror Follow Air Raids
Over Poor Areas

No Military Buildings Hit During Day

Canton, Sept. 25—(Reuter)—Reuter's correspondent made a personal tour today of the areas devastated by Japanese planes. Whole streets of poorer dwellings in the vicinity of Tungshan, the eastern suburb of Canton, had been literally torn asunder by the explosions of bombs.

In some places the corpses were as thick as flies on fly-paper, with limbs and mutilated bodies piled in the utmost confusion. Hundreds of weeping women were scrambling in the ruins for the remains of relatives while thousands more roamed the streets terror-stricken and bewildered, their minds partially deranged by the horrors of yesterday and today.

Reuter estimates that several thousand persons must have been killed or maimed, although it will be days, maybe weeks, before an accurate check can be accomplished.

Today's casualties dwarfed those in Shanghai on Bloody Saturday.

Foreign observers are puzzled over the nature of Japanese objectives, as not one Government building or military establishment was hit.

Most of the missiles had fallen in the densely packed dwelling areas of the poorer classes reducing the buildings and their occupants to mincemeat.

One ancient Chinese woman was killed while sitting at her front door. She still remained upright, quiet in death.

A grim-faced Chinese gentleman raised a piece of matting and displayed to Reuter's correspondent a mass of mangled remnants, saying simply: "This was my wife."

A children's school in the vicinity of Tungshan was completely demolished. Fortunately, because of the holidays, the occupants were few in number.

Allowing the populace no respite, Japanese planes subjected Canton to another two raids this morning. The first occurred at four o'clock, when a lone Japanese machine dropped five bombs. While en route to and returning from its objective, the plane flew low over Shameen, particularly when over the British bridge.

The second raid began at 8:30 o'clock. At least ten heavy bombers and a number of smaller fighters participated in the attack. The sky in all directions was brimful of aerial activity. Fights, bombings and the bursting of anti-aircraft shells presented an amazing spectacle against the clear blue morning sky. . . .

In a pamphlet issued by the Canton Committee for Justice to China, Dr. F. E. Bates, an American missionary doctor in charge of a hospital in the eastern suburbs of Canton, reveals that early in the afternoon of September 22 Japanese planes dropped six bombs on a residential area, killing about three hundred persons, mostly women and children. When the bombing stopped, Dr. Bates drove a truck to the scene and brought out many wounded and dying people.

We arrived at the scene of the bombing on September 22 within 20 minutes after the explosion, Dr. Bates declared. The "all clear" signal had not yet been given, but the disaster was evidently so great that at every turn police and soldiers had to facilitate our passage through the otherwise closed streets. The smoke and dust of the explosion had not yet cleared away, and the road for some distance was heavily piled with twisted timber, broken glass, bricks, plaster, and all manner of building material. As we approached the scene of the bombing, police and soldiers on every side were calling and beckoning us to the place where the wounded lay.

As soon as it became evident that a rescue party had arrived there came from every corner and hole in the debris which had, but a few moments before, been their living quarters, the most wretched, pitiable pieces of humanity that can be readily imagined. Some were seen, with blood dripping off their faces, crawling over the demolished buildings, calling loudly to their loved ones who were buried under the fallen structures.

One old lady, past eighty years of age, holding her bleeding head, called urgently to us to rescue her children and grandchildren who were buried in the mess beside her. Numerous children were running about in a semi-dazed way trying to find mothers who could be seen nowhere. One man, badly cut about the head and face, came out of a little hole where a bit of flooring from the upper storey had formed a triangle with the wall and floor below, carrying a little girl about ten years old. He pleaded with us to bring him back in the first load. His wife, two smaller children, and mother were buried under the houses and he seemed terribly fearful that something would happen to separate his only living child from him.

The story might be continued almost indefinitely, for the sights of those few moments, while we were filling the hospital cars with the wounded, were many indeed. We were but one of six hospitals which went to the rescue. Between groans of pains some were mourning for lost members of the family. Others whose families could all be accounted for had lost all of their worldly possessions. Where could they be able to pass the nights after leaving the hospital? Where could they get food?

The scenes of human pain and woe were almost innumerable and defy description. They were not living near a military camp, an arsenal, important railroad, or any kind of military defense works. It was one of the busy streets of this section of Canton, and yet the pitiless eye of the invader regarded not men. His was but a program of ruthless destruction and terror.

A general picture of Japanese aerial activity in South China appeared in the China Weekly Review, *Shanghai, on October* 30, 1937. *This summary follows, in part:*

HOW JAPANESE BOMBERS WREAK DESTRUCTION IN CANTON

CANTON, October 12—(Correspondence)—Villages of Kwantung Province, fishing and trading junks, the railways and industrial factories and the city of Canton, including unfortified areas of the city, are today the targets for Japanese bombing planes. . . . Those attacked . . . have no way to protect themselves from death by the Japanese fire. It is impossible to give the exact number of the Chinese dead and wounded. At a conservative estimate the Japanese bombs have killed a total of eight hundred persons in and about Canton, all of them civilians, some of them women and children, who, for the most part, have been killed in areas far removed from anti-aircraft guns.

The Japanese bombers, in addition to bombing residential sections and causing death and injury to many, have tried to destroy the Chung Sang University and the Sun Yat Sen Memorial Hall. The University has a group of beautiful, newly-erected buildings which have cost millions of dollars. Japanese bombers have tried to hit these buildings. Bombs have fallen in their vicinity but so far none of them have been hit.

In all there were fifty-six air raids on Canton up to Sept. 11. Planes have just come over my head as I am writing. This means that planes have threatened the city on an average of about twice a day for the last month.

The important Wuhan industrial center, commonly known as the "Chicago of the Orient," is composed of the three cities of Hankow, Wuchang, and Hanyang. The Wuhan cities are about seven hundred miles up the Yangtze River from Shanghai, and have a peacetime population of approximately one million.

On September 26, 1937, the North-China Daily News printed a Reuter report from Hankow which follows in full:

HANKOW TERROR IS HEIGHTENED BY NIGHT RAID

Hospital Workers Operate by Candle Light

Dreadful Carnage in Slum District

HANKOW, Sept. 25—(Reuter)—After the disastrous air-raid experienced in the afternoon, more death and destruction were caused in Hankow last night when Japanese planes revisited the city and dropped more bombs. The second attack lasted but ten minutes but during this brief period considerable havoc was created.

Every available Chinese doctor, dresser and nurse has been rounded up by the authorities, and the sufferings of the victims have been somewhat alleviated by the marvellous work of the Chinese Red Cross and the Methodist Mission Hospital, which threw open its doors to the dying and wounded.

Scores of operations and amputations were performed by candle light owing to the electric light system failing, while the very badly wounded received morphia to ease their terrible pains.

The morning revealed that an area measuring approximately 200 by 150 feet had been entirely reduced to a shambles, three bombs having landed within this space. Rescue work was still proceeding, and the debris were being sorted in search of further victims.

The most harrowing spectacle was witnessed by Reuter's correspondent when he made a tour of Wuchingmiao, the slum section of Hankow, after the first raid had converted the area into a charnel-house.

The streets in the district, only six feet wide, were fringed with poor hovels which collapsed like a pack of cards, burying their occupants as well as passers-by. Parts of bodies were strewn everywhere, which were gathered and piled up in heaps by rescue parties. More ghastly, however, was the occasional sight of an arm or leg waving feebly from beneath masonry which was too heavy to move without adequate apparatus.

Standing at a street corner for ten minutes, Reuter saw over 120 mangled bodies carried past, some moaning terribly, others completely lifeless. Particularly pathetic was the sight of stretchers bearing infant victims. All around the area the dead mingled with the dying. The majority of the injured were bleeding from gaping wounds and completely naked.

The proportion of children killed seemed inordinately large, presumably because most of them were indoors at the time. Tiny bodies seemed to outnumber those of adults.

Police, students and volunteers worked heroically under the most trying conditions, extricating the injured and removing the dead.

Many students appeared visibly exhausted late in the night but stuck to their grim task.

The Mayor, Mr. K. C. Wu, and other prominent Chinese officials personally directed operations and prevented wholesale confusion.

Rescue work was hampered by the failure of the electric lighting system and the lamentable shortage of doctors and ambulance workers, although the few available labored unceasingly.

Some ten thousand Chinese were living in Wuchingmiao when the raid occurred. It is stated that at the time of the bombing there was no Chinese soldier for miles around, while the arsenal, presumably the objective of the Japanese planes, is at least four miles distant.

Mass hysteria seized the occupants of a nearby Chinese girls' school as a result of the bombing. Girls ran hither and thither, shocked and demented by the terrible sights they had witnessed.

Besides Hankow, Hanyang and Wuchang also suffered from the raid. One of the bombs which fell in Hanyang struck a refugee camp, killing sixty and wounding a large number.

A bomb also narrowly missed the Wesleyan hospital in Hankow caring for hundreds of wounded.

Inordinately large fires were started where bombs dropped, and at a late hour last night most of these were still burning. Altogether nine Japanese planes took part in the raid, and of the bombs dropped two fell into the Yangtze, barely two hundred yards from the British river gunboat "Aphis."

Wuchingmiao, the slum district of Hankow, which was bombed yesterday, presented an even more tragic appearance after being re-visited by Japanese bombers today.

Thousands of bewildered, homeless victims wandered through the streets, while tired relief workers were still engaged in digging out victims, both dead and alive, some so badly mangled they were better dead than alive.

Reuter's correspondent encountered a ten-year-old Chinese boy bearing the slight corpse of his mother on his shoulders. He reverently laid her at the feet of a hospital gateman and asked that she be given a proper burial while he searched for his missing brothers and sisters.

Reuter's correspondent then looked into a hut and saw three men sitting upright in natural attitudes, all quite dead. One was clutching a dead child. In one room of another dwelling was a pile of corpses, while in the next room a Chinese woman was unconcernedly cooking a meal.

Chinese reports claim that one Japanese bomber was brought down forty kilometers from Hankow by Chinese pursuit planes after yesterday's raid.

It is estimated that the raiders came over at a height of two thousand feet, and foreign observers believe, they could not fail to notice the thickly populated conditions of Wuchingmiao and the absence of any military objectives.

Meanwhile, fearing another visitation, anxious watchers scanned the skies all day long.

CHAPTER VIII

ORGANIZED DESTRUCTION

THE PRECEDING CHAPTERS have dealt mainly with human injuries caused directly by the action of Japanese forces during and after their occupation of conquered territory and include only brief references to deliberate and systematic destruction, mainly by burning, after Japanese occupation of the areas involved had been completed. The organized destruction of homes and property in general, however, is of such vastness as to be little realized by the world at large.

Neutral foreign observers who have had the opportunity to travel extensively in the lower Yangtze River Delta since Japanese occupation of the areas state that destruction similar to that witnessed in and near Shanghai has occurred on an almost identical scale in the larger cities, such as Nanking, Wusih, Soochow and Chinkiang, no less than in the thousands of isolated groups of farmhouses which dot the countryside. These observers emphasize that, as at Shanghai, by far the greater proportion of this destruction is not the result of direct war operations but occurred *after* Japanese occupation.

The suffering caused directly by Japanese military excesses has thus been exacerbated by the destruction of countless homes and, more important, by the almost total annihilation of the means of production and means of existence in the case of hundreds of thousands, of those fortunate enough to have escaped direct military brutalities. Less poignant, perhaps, are the effects of these "indirect" causes, but for the population at large the destruction of their means of production and existence is even more telling than the rape and murder of tens of thousands of other victims.

Comprehensive data are of course not yet available, but at least in Shanghai itself—until the midsummer of 1937 China's chief industrial center—and to a lesser extent in other cities of the

ORGANIZED DESTRUCTION 119

Yangtze River Delta sufficient information has been collected to make possible estimates of the ravages caused by the war and subsequent destruction. The gradual opening, to a few foreigners at least, of the Shanghai International Settlement areas still under illegal occupation[1] by Japanese military forces has permitted detailed inspection of the effects of three months' fighting at Shanghai and has belatedly brought to light activities of the Japanese which had previously been more or less hidden from the general public. These activities will be described later.

SHANGHAI AND VICINITY

Probably the most accurate estimate to date of factory destruction in the Shanghai area is contained in the reports of the Industrial Section of the Shanghai Municipal Council of the International Settlement. A preliminary report of January 7, 1937, stated that the number of factories and workshops destroyed in the northern and eastern areas of the Settlement alone was 905, which, in normal times, employed a total of some 30,868 workers. These factories, the report states, were totally destroyed by fire. An additional number of about one thousand factories and workshops, large and small, have been more or less seriously damaged. "It is not possible to state the condition of these factories and workshops, but it is known that in some of the larger mills machinery has been rendered useless and would require replacement. . . . Evidence of disturbance and looting of factory premises is common. It is therefore assumed that none of these thousand plants could recommence operation."

The losses in the Shanghai Settlement constitute a minor part of the total destruction at Shanghai, for the larger industrial sections of Shanghai are located outside the borders of the Settlement and in such Chinese-administered territory as Chapei, Pootung, Jessfield, Nantao, Lunghwa, and similar districts. Chapei has been almost completely destroyed. This thickly populated area had in 1937 hardly recovered from the Sino-Japanese hostilities of 1932, which lasted for only a month, but caused losses estimated[2] at

[1] March, 1938. The Japanese forces have been in illegal occupation and control of the Hongkew, Yangtzepoo, Wayside, and other districts of the Shanghai International Settlement since August 14, 1937. This area comprises more than 33 per cent of the area of the Settlement.
[2] By the Shanghai General Chamber of Commerce.

about £100,000,000. Nantao, the old Chinese city of Shanghai, lies south of the French Concession and is another important Chinese industrial district. Relatively little fighting occurred there and Chinese troops had completely withdrawn from this area by the end of November 1937. There followed in December, January, February, and well into March, 1938, what Shanghai papers have described as "an orgy of burning." More than 80 per cent of the buildings in Nantao have been gutted by fires, almost all of which occurred after the Japanese occupation. Literally thousands of shops and factories have been completely destroyed. The Kiangnan Dock, a governmental enterprise which built the U.S.S. "Panay," has been almost completely destroyed. In Pootung, an industrial district on the banks of the Whangpoo River opposite Shanghai proper, similar devastation has occurred, including a large governmental alcohol plant, equipped with American machinery, which enjoyed a monopoly of production in this field in Central China.

Many columns could be filled with lists of fully or partially destroyed industrial establishments in and near Shanghai. The following Shanghai Municipal Council estimate, covering the International Settlement alone, will give some indication of the general destruction:

TYPE OF ENTERPRISE	NUMBER KNOWN COMPLETELY DESTROYED	NUMBERS OF WORKERS FORMERLY EMPLOYED
Woodworking	23	792
Furniture Manufacture	2	44
Metal Industry	72	1,241
Machinery and Metal Products	410	6,219
Vehicles	3	33
Bricks, Glass	8	405
Chemicals	49	564
Textiles	136	4,687
Clothing	44	3,476
Leather, Rubber	19	556
Food, Drinks, Tobacco	40	10,278
Printing, Paper, etc.	75	1,649
Scientific and Musical Instruments	3	140
Other Industries	21	784
	905	30,868

Commenting on this estimate, the American-owned *China Weekly Review*[1] observed:

"One can only make a wild guess at the average value of these manufacturing establishments, the greater variety of which were comparatively small and employed a limited number of workers. The manager of an American machinery house in Shanghai which supplied a great many of these plants informed the writer that these factories would probably run from U.S. $5,000 to $1,000,000; for example, the losses of the Nanyang Tobacco Factory, which previously used large quantities of American leaf tobacco, amounted to U.S. $660,000, covering the main factory buildings which were entirely destroyed. Then there is the matter of losses suffered by retail establishments and here again it is largely a matter of speculation. The officials of the Tax Department of the International Settlement think that a minimum of 100,000 retail shops have been destroyed and this also includes the homes and personal properties of most of the proprietors, who usually lived in rooms above the shops. Acres and acres of these little Chinese shops have either been destroyed by fire, air bombed or shelled by artillery or they were looted of their contents. One can drive through street after street in the Hongkew, Yangtzepoo, Chapei and Nantao districts and observe destruction on both sides extending for vast distances. Literally it seems that the wreckage extends for miles. In 1932 an area about a mile wide and two miles long was largely wiped out, but this time it seems that practically nothing escaped in an area estimated at more than three miles square. In many cases the destruction is practically indescribable. For example, hundreds of retail shops with living quarters above, located in the vicinity of the Administration Building of the Shanghai-Nanking-Hangchow Railway were so completely wrecked by continuous air bombardment that scarcely one brick was left standing on another.

"A Japanese visitor from Tokyo who accompanied the writer on a trip through this area was speechless with astonishment and only managed to catch his breath and exclaim: 'Just like our earthquake.' What he referred to was the devastating quake which almost wiped out Tokyo and Yokohama in 1923."

[1] *China Weekly Review*, Supplement, Shanghai, March 19, 1938.

The same issue of the *Review* also published the following estimate of losses in the Shanghai International Settlement north of Soochow Creek, the figures having been compiled by an American with a lengthy experience of trade and commercial activities in the Far East:

"Losses of industrial plant, equipment and property	yuan 350 million
" " other property	" 200 "
" " profits on yuan 250 million of import trade dropped in last 5 months of 1937	" 12.5 "
" " profits on yuan 100 million of export trade dropped in last 5 months of 1937	" 5 "
" on the shut-down in domestic industry and trade in the last 5 months of the year, possibly 8 times the losses of foreign trade	" 140 "
" " stocks of steel and iron and of scrap metal being taken away	" 13.4 "
" " charges and extra freights on 150,000 tons of Shanghai-bound cargo diverted to other ports and on adjustments in settlement of accounts	" 12.5 "
" " local contributions to refugee relief	" 1 "
Possible losses of goods destroyed or looted from warehouses in Hongkew and Yangtzepoo	" 50 "
Possible losses of household effects, general merchandise stocks, store fixtures, window glass, etc. etc., by looting and breakage in undestroyed properties in combat sections	" 50 "
Losses in freight haulage revenue in Shanghai shipping companies on unshipped exports abroad and on unshipped products of Shanghai industry to interior and coastal points, for five months at possibly yuan 2 million per month	" 10 "
Total	yuan 844.4 "

(Equivalent to approx. $281,466,000 in U.S. Currency.)"

ORGANIZED DESTRUCTION

The total losses up to mid-November 1937 of Greater Shanghai were estimated by foreign observers to exceed three billion Chinese dollars—almost three times the estimated losses caused by six weeks of hostilities at Shanghai in 1932.

In the table given immediately above are two items entered as "possible losses of goods destroyed or looted from warehouses in Hongkew and Yangtzepoo" and "possible losses of household effects, general merchandise . . . by looting and breakage in undestroyed properties in combat sections." These two items, totalling one hundred million Chinese dollars (about U.S. $33,000,000) consist of losses incurred almost exclusively as a result of organized Japanese looting or destruction. As early as October 1937 one could observe at Shanghai uniformed Japanese soldiers and Chinese laborers, most of them impressed workers, removing in a wholesale manner property consisting mainly of metals. In almost every case the property was loaded on to Japanese Army trucks and taken to Japanese controlled wharves along the Whangpoo River, where it was subsequently shipped to Japan on military transports. What property escaped damage from military operations was completely looted after the battle lines had left Shanghai. To this day[1] such looting continues.

Newspapers in Shanghai were flooded with protests against such organized looting, which nevertheless continued unabated. Foreigners frequently reported finding uniformed Japanese servicemen freely looting their homes despite the fact that these bore signboards reading: "This property is under the protection of the Special Japanese Naval Landing Party."

On January 31, 1937, the *Shanghai Evening Post* and the *North-China Daily News* published accounts of the wholesale theft of metal or "scrap-iron" from the Hongkew and Yangtzepoo districts which was shipped to Japan by supposedly reputable firms. According to the report in the *North-China Daily News* the scrap-iron was collected by coolies who claimed to be employed by the Japanese Residents' Association, but when a reporter for the paper attempted to photograph one of the dumps where the iron was being collected, he was attacked by Japanese "ronin" wearing semi-military uniforms. According to the *Evening Post* the Japanese removal of metal from

[1] March, 1938.

the areas controlled by the Japanese military forces began with the removal of sheet-iron from Chinese retail and wholesale iron shops along North Soochow Road. Later the Japanese iron collectors extended their activities to Chinese factories, where the machinery stocks were completely looted, including those of factories which had been burned. Still later the metal collectors began entering private homes or ruins of residences which had been burned and all pieces of metal, even hinges and locks of doors, were taken out. The article claimed that the machinery and other metals had been removed from some 1,000 Chinese factories large and small, one of the largest being the Nanyang Brothers cigarette plant on Yangtzepoo Road, which was struck by a shell and burned early in the war.

As already mentioned, the removal of machinery and metals from manufacturing establishments has been so extensive that complete replacements will be necessary before these concerns can resume operations. The amount of metal which the Japanese have removed from foreign and Chinese premises in the Shanghai areas alone can only be estimated, but it is thought to exceed greatly the figure of eighty thousand tons published in the Tokyo *Asahi*. Foreign merchants at Shanghai familiar with the metal trades claim that the scrap-iron which the Japanese have removed from the city or are in the process of removing, probably exceeds 100,000 tons.

In an editorial entitled "To What End?" in its issue of February 4, 1938, the *North-China Daily News* stated:

"The systematic removal of metals from the areas north of the Soochow Creek to which reference has already been made in the columns of this journal is giving rise to very considerable anxiety in the minds of neutral observers. The word 'systematic' is used advisedly, for gangs of Chinese coolies under a Chinese foreman, and controlled by Japanese, have for weeks past been making house-to-house, factory-to-factory visits on Chinese property removing not only metal which might be rightly termed scrap, but all types of metal fabrication from boilers down to small motors. The process which is going on hardly comes within the ordinary definition of looting where marauding soldiers take off what they can carry themselves, but amounts to the careful and systematic removal of every piece of metal which can be found on Chinese property. Obviously the Japanese are cleaning up the northern and eastern areas for the purpose of increasing their supply of scrap to be used for the manufacture of munitions and as a precautionary measure against any eventuality with which they may ultimately be faced. Actually compared with Japan's requirements the amount which can thus be taken away from Shanghai is not very imposing, but, in view of the hope that rehabilitation will soon be set afoot in Shanghai, the removal of essential machinery, which at no time could be put into operation, represents one of the cruelest blows which could be directed against the future prosperity of this port. Machinery costing lakhs of dollars for the manufacture of rubber goods, and for making textiles, down to the smallest motors for driving tool-making machines, steel bars weighing many tons down to the smallest pieces of metal costing but a few dollars are being taken out of Shanghai, and it is feared with every justification that Shanghai is being treated in a manner from which it will take decades to recover.

"It was recently stated on the authority of a Japanese journal that in the future Tientsin would take over many of the functions which have up to the present been carried out by Shanghai. Chinese factories which have escaped the effects of bombardment are being reduced to mere shells of brick and mortar. The ruins of those which have been destroyed are being thoroughly searched for whatever metal may still be found, and when the time comes for the Chinese to return to these areas they will find nothing with which to recommence their industrial activities. Two considerations are consequently involved. One is the often repeated assertion by the Japanese that they are conducting hostilities against the Nationalist Government and not against the Chinese people, and the other concerns the future prosperity of Shanghai. With regard to the former can it be suggested for one moment that this organized plunder of one of Shanghai's most important industrial areas can be carried out without the humble Chinese themselves suffering? The question has but to be asked to answer itself. The Chinese industrialist is being made to suffer in his pocket as so many of his nationals have suffered in their bodies. The businesses which have been laboriously built up during the past ninety years or so, are being ruthlessly destroyed, and the flourishing districts of Wayside and Yangtzepoo are being reduced to mere shadows of their former opulence. It may be argued that shipping is the foundation of this port's fortunes. That is undoubtedly true, but the undertakings which have been created during all these years are just as necessary for Shanghai's well being as is the seaborne trade in which she figures so largely. In face of these things how can it be said that these hostilities are not being waged against the Chinese people?

"This journal would be failing in its duty to Shanghai if it did not register the most emphatic protest possible. The matter concerns practically every neutral in Shanghai, as well as the Japanese themselves, and may be expected to have serious repercussions upon the fortunes of this great city. The organized spoliation of the areas in question must of necessity have a direct bearing upon the trade which has brought the foreign community to these shores, for without a prosperous Chinese community that trade would be impossible. The sterilization of these industrial districts will have a profound effect upon the future revenue of the municipality. And so it follows that not only are the interests of unoffending Chinese being damaged, but those foreign interests, the scrupulous respect for which has been so often promised, are being damaged to an extent which it is at present impossible to estimate. Let there be no mistake about it; it is not only mere scrap that is being removed from Wayside and Yangtzepoo; Chinese installations of machinery are being dismantled for export to Japan. The wherewithal for ultimate rehabilitation is being taken away, and when the Chinese are allowed ultimately to return to these areas of desolation they will find themselves faced with the enormous task of building their undertakings from the bare ground up again. There can be none of that failure to understand the Japanese in this manner. The facts speak for themselves, and Shanghai is entitled to ask the question with which this article is headed. What is the purpose of stripping these areas of Shanghai of all that is necessary for a portion of the rehabilitation of this port, unless it is an endeavor permanently to disable? It may be argued that it is a form of reprisals for what was done to Japanese concerns in Tsingtao. What was done there this journal just as emphatically reprobated, and the considerations which applied in that instance just as closely apply in this. So much has already been done toward reducing these districts to mere skeletons of their original industrial proportions that considerable disaster has already been wrought. It is to be hoped that even now the Japanese authorities will hold their hands, for it must be apparent to them that a prosperous Shanghai is just as essential for them as it is for those Chinese and foreign interests which are being placed in such grave peril by a perfectly incomprehensible procedure."

The *Shanghai Evening Post* on January 24, 1938, printed this denunciation of Japanese looting at Shanghai: "Chinese properties in Hongkew and Yangtzepoo are reported by foreign observers to have been subject, over a period stretching back virtually to the commencement of hostilities and reaching to the present day, to steady and large-scale removal by Japanese.

"We wish at this time to ask how such conduct can be squared with official Japanese assurances that there is intended to be no confiscation of Chinese belongings save in certain special instances involving Chinese close to or in the Government or otherwise deemed guilty of leadership in China's resistance to Japan.

"If there is any doubt in the mind of responsible Japanese officials that things are as stated—that goods and equipment are being taken under Japanese supervision or by Japanese direct, without sanction of the proper Chinese owners, from godowns, factories and homes— that doubt, we believe, could quickly be set at rest by the most cursory of observation first-hand or inquiry among foreigners whose business connections have given them a special interest in the matter. Such ingenuous amaze as was registered at last Saturday's press conference may serve to keep spokesmen legalistically clear of commitments, but it shows no sincere desire to get at the truth. Chinese are not allowed access to their properties; foreigners, even when they see with their own eyes, and detailed lists of looted Chinese properties are kept, are reluctant to become embroiled in disputes which are not primarily theirs.

"But the facts are so widely known, and for the matter of that there are so many foreign victims of the same activities, that we doubt if they will be disputed. And if they are admitted, what justification can be brought forward?

"It has been stated that a formal authorization has been given the

Japanese Residents' Association to loot Chinese properties as partial recompense for their own individual losses. Frankly we don't know anything about that save the report, and when the report was carried to a Japanese spokesman it was denied. So we have nothing definite about how organized and authorized the removals may be. Yet we know of the removals, we know that the Japanese authorities could prevent them, and as the circumstances stand they constitute a clear and obvious violation of what we have been told concerning 'no confiscation.'

"Perhaps the statement with reference to confiscation had to do with passage of title to real estate. But the principle involved is certainly the same if a factory is handed over bodily to the Japanese, or if—as we know to be the case—damaged but still valuable machinery is removed from that factory, leaving it a useless shell. When it comes to such property of immediately marketable value as, for example, cotton from godowns, there is only one word for unauthorized seizure and removal and that word is theft.

"Foreigners are now allowed freely in Hongkew and Yangtzepoo which presumably has brought a halt to any further large-scale removal of their goods. But Chinese are not thus freely allowed in, even yet, and they are helpless even to survey the situation of their properties. To take advantage of that situation seems to us without any excuse whatever and, as stated, completely to be in violation of the expressed official Japanese position."

Such comments were apparently unheeded by the Japanese, and the *Shanghai Evening Post* on February 3, 1938, again attacked the continued pillaging in an editorial entitled "Robbing China's Poor":

"There can be no possible argument save that of a desire wholly to exterminate the people of China—an extreme view which even the most violent of Japanese spokesmen have avoided—for policies of continuously depriving those people from the means of livelihood.

"Far from enunciating such a view, General Matsui[1] and Admiral Hasegawa[2] have made generous personal contributions to

---

[1] General Iwane Matsui, then Commander-in-Chief of Japanese forces in the Yangtze Delta area.

[2] Admiral Hasegawa, Commander-in-Chief of Japanese Naval Forces in Chinese waters.

Chinese refugee relief in Shanghai. Other leading Japanese have repeatedly declared that Japan has no animosity toward the Chinese people.

"Yet daily in Hongkew and Yangtzepoo, observers see continued Japanese removals of machinery from Chinese factory properties, while Chinese owners and workers are alike debarred even from access to those properties.

"We do not refer, now, to the removal of damaged machinery from buildings which have been shelled and burned. Such removal is an unjustified confiscation but it is far less serious than the removal of sound machinery, in working condition. This latter act is virtually the taking of rice from the mouths of hungry workers, now unemployed and placed more or less permanently in that category through the gutting of their places of former employment.

"Of course any such unauthorized removal is plain theft. But when it entails an elimination of the means of employment until such time as Hongkew and Yangtzepoo may be freely opened once more, it is something worse, for it contributes to the starvation of innocent men, women and children.

"If there is anything that can be said for the Japanese position in this matter we shall be glad to hear of it. Does anyone doubt the facts, to begin with? And the facts granted, is Japan's need for metal a sufficient extenuation for this piratical activity which after all can hardly decide a war's issue, but which certainly has a most vital bearing on the welfare of helpless factory workers quite apart from the rights of the property-owners themselves?"

IN THE YANGTZE RIVER VALLEY

Little statistical data is available regarding destruction and looting which is known to have occurred in other areas. Some indication of its extent has already been given in earlier chapters.

According to the *China Weekly Review*,[1] " . . . the destruction in Shanghai has been duplicated in innumerable towns and villages of the Shanghai Delta region of which Shanghai is the chief city and metropolis. Within a radius of 100 miles from Shanghai there are no less than twelve large cities with an aggregate population of

[1] The *China Weekly Review*, Shanghai, Supplement, March 19, 1938.

5,000,000. All of these cities have suffered extensive war damage, not to mention the losses of smaller towns and villages in the area. For example, the industrial city of Wusih, located about 100 miles north-west of Shanghai, contained a population of 900,000. Its manufacturing establishments suffered heavy damages or complete destruction as a result of Japanese air-bombing operations. Losses included the destruction or serious damage to several flour mills, one cotton mill, one power-plant and a highly modernized silk filature which produced the finest grade of silk hosiery yarn for the American stocking trade. Another town, Kashing, located in the center of an important silk producing area in Chekiang province with 450,000 population, was devastated and completely evacuated. Another town, Sungkiang, about 25 miles from Shanghai, with a population of about 200,000, was almost wiped out. The city of Soochow, a rich and conservative metropolis located about fifty miles from Shanghai, suffered a drop in population from 350,000 to less than 500 people when the Japanese occupied the walled area."

The *Review* quotes part of a letter written by a foreign motorist, who had completed a trip from Shanghai to Wusih, passing through Taitsang, Changshu, Soochow, and Quinsan, to the *North-China Daily News:*

"Nearly all villages near the road are burned or destroyed by bombing. Not a single chicken, duck or goose was seen during the entire trip. Farmers were working in the fields and numerous parties of country people under Japanese military overseers were mending the roads. All destroyed bridges have been restored.

"Just before reaching Wusih, the road passes through the once busy market town of Toongding. This town shows the most appalling destruction. There is hardly a house standing. A few people were seen picking among the ruins for the salvage of such articles as had escaped fire and shell.

"At Wusih the northern suburbs for a mile were burned, as were all cotton mills excepting one. Many silk hongs and warehouses suffered a similar fate. Hotels, shops, godowns and residences in the area between the railway station and city wall were destroyed. The railway station and city wall were destroyed. The railway stations and freight godowns are in ruins. Telephone and electric wires are down.

"On entering the city the same destruction is to be noted. It is estimated that at least half the buildings in Wusih have been burned. This includes all of the shopping district from the centre of the city to the north gate and from the north gate on out to the long iron bridge which spans the Grand Canal, on the road to Weishan. The long street which runs parallel with the Grand Canal, south of the city, for a distance of a mile has been burned on both sides. This city, which was once a great manufacturing center and grain depot, lies prostrate."

Eye-witness accounts given elsewhere in this volume have attested that burning and looting were carried out by uniformed Japanese officers and soldiers and that loot was removed by Japanese army trucks. Japanese "ronin"—the equivalent in English would be, approximately, "gangster"—took up where the military left off.

"It is this type of gangster—hangers-on of the Army—who is responsible for the systematic looting of Chinese and foreign properties located in territories now under control of the Imperial Japanese Army," says the *China Weekly Review*.[1] "The published reports of murders, lootings and rapings for which uncontrolled soldiers of the Imperial Army were responsible in such places as Nanking, Soochow, Hangchow and Wuhu, have been repeated in hundreds of villages and towns by gangs of so-called ronin who have literally 'cleaned out' this section of China of everything of value which the unfortunate Chinese people were unable to carry with them when they fled en masse to points of safety in the interior of the country. . . ."

"At many points up and down the China coast, particularly in Kiangsu, Chekiang and Fukien provinces, one finds monuments which have been erected in honour of local military commanders or provincial rulers of previous decades who have been successful in defeating pirates who have ravaged the coast and in some cases seized cities and held them for heavy ransoms. There is a monument of this character standing on a hill near the town of Nantungchow, about eighty miles up the Yangtze from Shanghai. The inscription on the

[1] *China Weekly Review*, Shanghai, Ferbuary 5, 1938.

Nantungchow monument states that it was erected in honor of a heroic Chinese commander who defeated a gang of pirates which had operated in the Lower Yangtze for many years. The pirate gang was composed of Japanese. Most of the other monuments of similar character that one finds up and down the coast also commemorate victories over Japanese piratical gangs. One is reminded of the similarity of the present Japanese invasion of the China coast! Despite all of the propaganda about the 'holy war,' 'pan-Asiaism,' 'economic cooperation,' 'anti-Communism,' the evidence is increasing that Japan's present expedition is not a war in the accepted 'undeclared' sense of the word, but only another pillaging and piratical expedition on a somewhat grander scale than previous adventurers of this character. If the Japanese had any idea of correcting long-standing abuses in the relations of the two nations or assisting the Chinese people to improve their political and economic status in the world as an independent nation, it is obvious that the Japanese Government would not permit its soldiery and citizens to engage in the orgies of murder, rape, looting, and incendiarism which have characterized this Japanese invasion of the China coast. These activities are not the normal manifestations of a nation of the 20th century imbued with altruistic and humanitarian ideals of helpfulness toward a weaker neighboring people. They are the actions of a nation still steeped in the traditions and barbaric conceptions of nationalistic aggrandisement as typified in European colonial policies of a bygone age.

"The Japanese have always boasted of their knowledge of Chinese history—in fact their present belief in the Divine Origin of the Emperor is an adaptation of the political theories of the Chou kings (1100 to 300 B.C.) who succeeded the Shang dynasty. The Chou kings regarded their wars against the Shang emperor as 'Decreed by Heaven,' and their attempt to conquer the then Asiatic world as the carrying out of a Divine Command. But while the Japanese have borrowed the terminology, they have seemingly failed to comprehend the political philosophy which the Chinese developed to a high degree even in the Shang dynasty (1750 to 1100 B.C.)—that military conquest always fails where it is impossible to enlist the loyalty and cooperation of the population. World experience has demonstrated that it is impossible to rule a hostile people permanently by means of military garrisons, yet the Japanese are following that method of procedure exactly by planning to break the country up into small principalities to be ruled by Japanese armies. Although the Japanese have, through long preparation, demonstrated their military superiority over the Chinese armies, the Japanese have been unable to prevent their victories from degenerating into looting raids comparable to the actions of the barbarous tribes of the North and North-west which used to harass the Chinese Empire. Chinese civilization and political philosophy have survived because of the widespread belief among the Chinese people that rulers were appointed by Heaven to bring about the welfare of mankind and the promotion of the public good. While the Japanese have had much to say about the holy nature of their campaign, the actions of their uncontrolled soldiery and ronin adventurers have created the impression that the whole enterprise is nothing more nor less than the machinations of the devil.

"European political control as exemplified in colonial administrations in Oriental lands persisted because European colonial administrators learned to apply, in limited measure we admit, the political philosophies of the early Chinese sages. Thus they ceased to be regarded as bands of uncouth barbarian adventurers intent upon destroying Chinese civilization and culture and in time ceased to be regarded as hateful tyrants intent only upon gorging themselves on the spoils of war and the sweat of the enslaved population. But the Japanese failure to comprehend the inwardness of Chinese civilization was matched only by their equal inability to understand the reasons for the persistence of European colonial administrations on the Asiatic coast. The result has been the inevitable degeneration of Japan's 'holy war' into a sordid pillaging expedition not greatly differing, except in extent, from the activities of piratical gangs which harassed the China coast in earlier days."

All of this deliberate destruction, looting, and burning of Chinese property from modern factory to peasant hovel is another phase of the Japanese terror in China. It is in this fashion that Japan makes war upon the "obstinate Chinese Government" and the "lawless Chinese army."

CONCLUSION

IN THE PRECEDING chapters I have confined myself largely to introducing the eye-witness accounts which, together with a few press agency and newspaper reports, form the bulk of this volume. I now add some general observations based upon this material, supplemented by personal experience gained in the course of nearly twenty years spent in the Far East.

Fragmentary accounts of the Japanese invasion of China and of the occupation of the Yangtze Delta and ultimately Nanking itself have found their way into the newspapers. It may be questioned, however, whether it was generally realized that the reports of rape and loot and general bestiality flashed over the cables could be supported by signed eye-witness accounts collected from unimpeachable sources, by authentic photographs, by films, and by official documents. All doubts as to the existence of such material should be dispelled by the publication of a selection of it in the present volume.

The wealth of evidence here given nevertheless represents only a cross-section of happenings which were an integral part of the Japanese invasion. It has been necessary to reject a great deal of similarly well documented material because of space requirements. The reader should bear in mind that the reports contained herein cover a relatively few large centers where neutral foreign observers chanced to be stationed. The happenings in rural areas of occupation as a whole, directly affecting as they did the agrarian population which constitutes more than 80 per cent of the total population of China, would fill a volume by themselves. At the same time, little mention is made in this book of such attendant factors as the systematic destruction of educational institutions such as the well-known Nankai University in Tientsin with the evident intention of annihilating the sources of higher education in China.

Apart from vague suggestions of exaggeration, the Japanese authorities have not denied that outrages were committed at Nanking and elsewhere by the Japanese army. In strict privacy, Japanese civilians of the better sort have admitted with deeply felt shame that the reports were substantially true. By official apologies the defense put forward appears to be (*a*) that these were but isolated incidents and (*b*) that the same sort of thing has happened in other wars. "Granted," says a recent Japanese pamphlet,[1] "that certain atrocities have been committed by Japanese troops and that certain incidents have arisen between Japanese troops and foreigners, let us say for comparison that such cases involve say 0.1 per cent, or 0.5 per cent, or even 1 per cent, of the Japanese forces on Chinese soil. Taking the highest figure of 1 per cent, does that constitute an 'enormous' percentage of 'bad characters' among the Japanese troops when such troops number several hundred thousand men? The answer is plain to all fair-minded persons."

This line of argument is reminiscent of the maid-servant who sought to excuse her baby on the ground that "it was only a little one." In view of the large number of well substantiated cases reported it is evident that considerably more than 1 per cent of the Japanese forces in China, which would mean between four thousand and five thousand men were involved. One ventures to hope that our own British High Command would be concerned over the fact that five thousand troops had run amuck to the extent revealed in the foregoing pages. And their concern would surely be heightened by the knowledge that many of the outrages took place under the observed direction of army officers.

To suggest that the widespread violence reported in these pages with a wealth of authentic detail still represents only the exception to the rule and that for this reason one should close one's eyes to the horrors of war and the proverbial brutality of the soldiery would be to deny the very foundations of justice and ethics. If cruelty is the exception then it should be all the easier to protest against what has happened and show our abhorrence of it; if it is the rule then it is all the more necessary to prevent its repetition. Indeed, it is surely the current tendency to condone monstrosities by such arguments that is one of the most dangerous influences dragging the world back

[1] "Plain Speaking on the Sino-Japanese Conflict. Shanghai 1937-38. 10.—Mountains out of Mole-Hills."

to anarchy. What we need is *unconditional* allegiance to law, decency, and morality, for their own sakes, and not allegiance to them only if the other fellow will subscribe to them too. Such allegiance is not allegiance, and certainly not morality, at all.

Those who try to explain away these facts with the threadbare excuse that all wars have yielded their crop of horrors tend to forget that Japan's primary offence against international decency is the fact that she is making war upon China at all. The calculated brutalities which have accompanied the war simply make that offence just so much the more serious.

Probably it will have occurred to some readers to question how far the outrages committed by the Japanese army in China were simply the result of troops running wild in the heat of victory or how far they may have represented a policy of deliberate terrorism on the part of the Japanese authorities. The facts of the case point to the latter conclusion. Military excesses are understandable, though still not excusable, where they occur immediately after the occupation of a city, especially when the occupation comes at the end of a wearisome campaign. But in Nanking, however, to quote an outstanding example, outrages by Japanese soldiery went on for three months after the occupation of the city and were still continuing when the writer left China early in April, 1938.

One is thus forced to conclude either that a considerable section of the Japanese army was out of control or that it was the wish of the Japanese High Command to strike terror into the hearts of the Chinese people in the hope that thereby the latter would be cowed into submission.

Either conclusion is equally painful, but there is no evading the choice. Nor does there seem reason to doubt that precisely similar treatment would be meted out to any country which the Japanese army might invade.

This age is supposed to have seen the awakening of the Japanese nation, highly civilized by its contacts with the West, yet boasting of an ancient culture. But in this very supposition lies the root of the troubles with which the Far East is now beset.

In his very able book *The Far Eastern Crisis,* the one-time American Secretary of State, Henry L. Stimson, says: "To the American

Government Japan was a friendly, powerful, and sensitive neighbor which, within a short space of a single human lifetime, had emerged from the isolation of feudal military autocracy into a modern industrialized state. Under the guidance of a very far-sighted group of elder statesmen she had assimilated with extraordinary rapidity the material elements of Western civilization. Her energetic and intelligent people had made gigantic strides in the technical arts, in manufactories, and in commerce. This industrial development was also gradually resulting in liberalism in social and political ideas. Japan had adopted a constitution with parliamentary features and she had been extending the suffrage among her people."

Thus did Japan appear not only to the American Government but also to the peoples and governments of all Western nations. Many Chinese, too, held this view. But this is a false assumption stemming from a superficial observation of the facts and upon this error rests the whole common concept of Far Eastern politics. In the pages that follow the quotation given above, Mr. Stimson adds: "The basic inheritance of the virtues and weaknesses of militarism had been only partially modified by the developing economic and social conditions of the industrial revolution and the ideas of Western democracy which had come with it, and their government still reflected these two elements, as yet imperfectly blended and each striving for mastery."

The modern industrialized state of which Mr. Stimson speaks is in cold reality only a vehicle for the feudal military autocracy which is Japan. Japan's common people, be they peasants or factory workers, have today almost as little say in the control of their destinies as at any time in the history of Japan. Japan is ruled by her militarists in alliance with the great family trusts which control the economic life of the country. The people have no democratic rights and liberties since the Diet is powerless; there is neither free speech nor a free press, and it is a criminal offence even to *think* that the Constitution—which gives absolute power to the Emperor—should be altered. Anyone who ventures to speak against the war goes to prison, as witness the arrests of hundreds of liberal professors, authors, journalists and teachers and of two Labor M.P.s in December, 1937, and February, 1938, for having "spread anti-war talk."

Wars of aggression are the time-honored remedy employed by Japan's ruling class for social discontents. So long as the myth of prosperity through easy conquest is believed, the semi-feudal land-owning-militarist caste can hope to stave off agrarian reform and preserve its economic and political power. So long as aggression is supported by the big business interests there is unity of aim amongst those who hold power. If, however, aggression became both dangerous and unprofitable; if, in particular, economic pressure were exerted by Britain and the U.S.A. upon Japan, there would almost certainly be a split between the militarists and the plutocracy which would enable the Japanese people to win their freedom and stop the war. The mass of the Japanese people have nothing to gain, and much to lose, in this war. They are dying and being wounded while their families suffer from rising prices, longer hours of labor and a growing dearth of the necessities of life. Wounded soldiers are kept from talking to their relatives by not being allowed to see them alone, and a severe censorship prevents the Japanese people from knowing that Chinese resistance is stubborn and the war likely to go on a long time. The Government is afraid that if the truth were known the morale of the civilian population would weaken.

The financiers and big industrialists who realize their vital dependence on Britain and America would want to call a halt to aggression if we cut down their profits through a boycott and made it so difficult for Japan to buy war materials that only the totalitarian economic policies of the military could enable Japan to fight at all. Big business in Japan is far from powerless but supports the war so long as it appears profitable and not dangerous to itself.

What has happened, and is still happening, in China is something which must concern us all—advocates of collective security and isolationists alike. It is my fervent hope that the story of China's present travail and especially of those noble men and women at Nanking and elsewhere whose experiences have been recounted in the foregoing pages will serve as an inspiration to all who have at heart the cause of international justice. Surely China cannot be allowed to succumb unless mankind is prepared to renounce for many generations to come its right to decide between right and wrong and is willing to risk the repetition of such unspeakable horrors as China is suffering today.

CONCLUSION

"What can we do?" is the helpless cry of our fear-ridden governing groups. Practically, and as an immediate step, we can begin to implement our oft-repeated pledges by helping China with arms or, if that is not feasible, with financial aid. But action must not be allowed to stop there. There can be no hope of peace for any of us unless we can set up and maintain some permanent system of collective security which will protect peace-loving nations against aggression. The shadow of war will not be removed until we begin to realize that, as Hendrik Willem van Loon has pointed out in one of his books, we are all of us fellow-passengers on the same planet and the weal and woe of everybody else means the weal and woe of ourselves.

APPENDICES

APPENDIX A

CASE REPORTS COVERING CHAPTERS II AND III

THE FOLLOWING CASES of disorder, or worse, were recorded by foreign observers and reported to the Japanese authorities over roughly the same period as that covered by Chapters I and II, namely, from the entry of the Japanese on December 13 up to the end of the year.

The cases originally filed, numbering 170, were only a selection of those coming under the notice of the Zone Committee. Although probably true, the majority of the reports were not capable of ready verification and therefore were withheld. The present selection has been made with a view to avoiding wearisome repetitions of the same type of report. A similar procedure has been adopted in connection with Appendix B and Appendix C.

For the convenience of the reader the cases have been rearranged in chronological order but the original case numbers have been retained. It is to be noted that the incidents thus recorded cover only the Nanking Safety Zone, and that the rest of Nanking was practically deserted until the end of January and most of the time was without foreign observers during this whole period.

While a sufficient number of these cases were observed by foreigners to make clear what was going on, other cases were reported to these observers by Chinese co-workers, whose veracity there was no reason to doubt. For each case so reported, a written statement in Chinese was called for and a translation made into English. This accounts for the peculiar style employed in some of the case reports: the English versions had been written under such pressure that no time could be taken to polish up the text.

Case No.

5. On the night of December 14 there were many cases of Japanese soldiers entering Chinese houses and raping women or taking them away. This created a panic in the area and hundreds of women moved into the Ginling College Campus yesterday. Consequently, three American men spent the night at Ginling College last night to protect the three thousand women and children in the compound.

6. On December 14 about thirty Japanese soldiers with no apparent leader searched the University Hospital and the nurses' dormitory. The staff of the Hospital were systematically looted, the objects taken were: six fountain pens, $180.00, four watches, two hospital bandages, two flashlights, two pairs of gloves, one sweater.

10. At noon, December 14, on Chien Ying Hsiang Road, Japanese soldiers entered a house and took four girls, raped them, and let them return in two hours.

15. On December 15, Japanese soldiers entered a Chinese house on Hankow Road and raped a young wife and took away three women. When two husbands ran after them, the soldiers shot both of them.

1. On December 15, six street sweepers of the second division of the Sanitary Commission of the Safety Zone were killed in the house they occupied at Kuleo and one seriously injured with a bayonet by Japanese soldiers. No apparent reason whatever, these men were our employees. The soldiers entered the house.

4. On the night of December 15, seven Japanese soldiers entered the University of Nanking Library building and took seven Chinese women refugees, three of whom were raped on the spot.

7. On December 15, everyone of our large refugee camps in public and institutional buildings reported that the Japanese soldiers had been there and robbed the refugees several times.

8. On December 15, the American Ambassador's residence was broken into and searched and some small personal articles taken.

APPENDIX A

The following cases were filed with the Japanese authorities under covering letters some of which are reproduced in Appendix D (Doc. Z 8 and 13):

Case No.
16. On December 15, a man came to the University Hospital with a bayonet wound and reported that six Chinese men were taken from the Safety Zone to carry ammunition to Hsiakwan and when they got there the Japanese soldiers bayoneted them all. He however survived and got back to the University of Nanking Hospital.
17. On the 15 December, at about 8:00 a.m., according to a report by a Chinese Wang Yuhwei of the (German) Ho Tzon Chi Liang Ho Kung Sze at 6 Fu Kan, some Japanese soldiers came to their place. They seized him and upon presentation of his German registration, they threw it on the ground. He also claims they tore down the German flag displayed there. He was conscripted to carry a load to the Chuin Kuan Hsieh Shao after which he was released and given the slip showing he had done work. On his way home while on Kiukiang Road he was shot twice from behind without any apparent reason by another Japanese soldier or soldiers. He is now in the University Hospital, where he may be interviewed.
18. On the night of December 15, a number of Japanese soldiers entered the University of Nanking buildings at Tao Yuen and raped thirty women on the spot, some by six men.
19. On December 15 a man came to the University Hospital. He had been carrying his 60-year-old uncle into the Safety Zone and soldiers shot his uncle and wounded himself.
20. On the night of December 16, seven Japanese soldiers broke windows; robbed refugees, wounded University staff member with bayonets because he had no watch or girls to give them; raped women on the premises.
22. On the night of December 16 Japanese soldiers beat several of the Zone policemen near the University of Nanking demanding that they provide girls for the soldiers from among the refugees.

23. On December 16, Japanese soldiers carried off fourteen Red Swastika workers at Wutaishan.
24. On December 16, Japanese soldiers took a cooking kettle from workers of the soup kitchen of the Red Swastika Society,[1] dumping the rice in the kettle on the ground.
27. On December 16, Japanese soldiers entered the residence of our chief sanitary inspector at 21 Kuling Road, and took motorcycles, one garbage bucket and five bicycles.
29. On December 16, Japanese soldiers tried to take the ambulance from University Hospital and were only prevented by prompt arrival of an American member of the Committee, the Rev. John Magee.
47. On the night of the 16th at 8 o'clock two Japanese officers and two soldiers came to No. 18 Kan Ho Yen. They drove out the men in the house. Some women neighbors ran away. Those who remained in the house (who could not get away) were raped. The vest of one of the soldiers was left in the house.
57. On December 16, seven girls (ages ranged from sixteen to twenty-one) were taken away from the home at the Military College. Five returned. Each girl was raped six or seven times daily—reported December 18. On December 17 at 11 p.m. soldiers climbed over the wall and took away two girls but they returned them in thirty minutes.
33. On December 17, Japanese soldiers went into Lo Kai Lu No. 5, raped four women, took one bicycle, bedding and other things. They disappeared quickly when Hatz and myself appeared on the spot.
37. On December 17, in a small house behind my house at Siao Tao Yuen, Can Ho Yueh, a woman was raped and stabbed. If she gets medical aid today she can probably be saved. The woman's mother was badly beaten over the head.
41. On Dec 17 near Judicial Yuan a young girl after being raped was stabbed by a bayonet in her abdomen.

[1] A Chinese charitable organization equivalent to Red Cross Societies in Europe and America.

APPENDIX A 147

42. On December 17 at Sian Fu Wua a woman of 40 years was taken away and raped.
45. On December 17 many women were taken away from a primary school at Wu Tai Shan and raped for the whole night and released the next morning.
46. On December 17 at the Wu Kyia home garden three men were killed, and two women were taken away and cannot be found.
48. On December 17, Wang Yu-chien, Inspector of the 4th Division of the Housing Commission, at 4 Hsu Pu Hsiang reported soldiers entered daily, robbed and looted. Wife and two boys fled to Ginling College. Mother and boy remained. Wang threatened so he had to leave.
53. At 3 p.m. on December 17, three girls at No. 10 Ta Fang Hsiang Refugee's Home were raped by Japanese soldiers in turn. Also one woman was seriously wounded by a shot.
86. On December 17, three girls belonging to Mr. Y. H. Shaw's family (Executive Secretary of the Y.M.C.A.) were taken from the Military College, where they had removed from 7 Ying Yang Ying for safety. They were taken to Kwoh Fu Road, raped, and sent back at midnight by Japanese soldiers.
94. On the night of December 17, eleven refugee women were taken from the Ginling College Campus by Japanese soldiers while an officer in charge of a searching party had the staff lined up at the front gate for over an hour. The officer tore up the letter certifying the Institution had been searched before.
95. On December 17 the daughter-in-law of a refugee family living on the Ginling College Campus was raped in her room. The daughter of one of the teachers was carried off by Japanese soldiers.
54. On December 18 about 5 p.m. some ten soldiers entered and took all the bedding and other belongings of 100 refugees and sanitary staff including our chief of staff, Mr. Ma Sen.
55. On December 18, evening, 450 terrified women fled for shelter

to our office and spent the night in our yard. Many have been raped.

56. On December 18, 4 p.m. at No. 18 I-Ho Road Japanese soldiers wanted some cigarettes and when he hesitated the soldier smashed the side of his head with a bayonet. The man is now at the University Hospital and is not expected to live.

59. On December 18, while Major Y. Nagai was kind enough to call on our Chairman, Mr. Rabe, at his house at Siao Tao Yuen, a neighbor right opposite called for help because four Japanese soldiers had entered his house and one of them was raping one of the women. Major Nagai caught the man and slapped his face and ordered him out. The other three soldiers ran when they saw the Major coming.

62. On December 18, refugee Home at Military College reports: On the 16th two hundred men were taken away and only five returned; on the 17th twenty-six men were taken away; on the 18th, thirty men were taken away. Looting: money, luggage, and one bag of rice, over four hundred sheets of hospital beddings, one man was killed (age twenty-five), one old woman was knocked down and died after twenty minutes.

74. On December 18, Dr. Bates found a Japanese soldier in the University of Nanking building at Siao Tao Yuen where his own office is located and asked him what he was doing. The soldier threatened Dr. Bates with his pistol.

63. Reported on December 18—on Ninghai Road half a tin of kerosene oil was taken away from a boy by force and the boy savagely beaten when asked to carry same. At Pin Chen Shan No. 6 one pig was taken away by Japanese soldiers. A number of ponies have been taken away by five Japanese soldiers. Several girls living in No. 12 I-Ho Road were raped after chasing all the men away who lived together with them as refugees. One tea-house master's daughter, age seventeen years, was raped by seven Japanese soldiers and she died on the 18th. Last night three Japanese soldiers raped four girls between 6 and 10 o'clock. In No. 5 Moh Kan Road one old man reported his daughter was brutally raped by several Japanese soldiers. Three girls were taken away by Japanese soldiers last night

from Girls' College and returned to No. 8 Tao Ku Sing Tsuen in bad condition this morning. In Pin An Shang, a girl was raped by three Japanese soldiers and died. Raping, robbery and searching are occurring at T Yang Ying.

64. Reported on December 18—there are about 540 refugees crowded in Nos. 83 and 85 on Canton Road. Since the 13th instant up to the 17th those houses have been searched and robbed many times a day by Japanese soldiers in groups of three to five. Today the soldiers are looting the places mentioned above continually. At present, women of younger ages are forced to go with the soldiers every night by sending motor-trucks to take them. They are released the next morning. More than thirty women and girls have been raped. The women and children are crying the whole nights through. Conditions inside the compound are worse than can be described.

60. On December 19 at 11:30 a.m., Mr. Hatz reports that he found two Japanese soldiers in a dugout at the house next door to our Headquarters on Ninghai Road, who were trying to rape some of the women. There were twenty women in the dugout. Hearing the women yelling for help, Mr. Hatz went into the dugout and chased the soldiers out.

66. On December 19 (outside Zone but observed by Director). Yesterday it was reported to me that the residence of Mr. Douglas Jenkins, Jr., Third Secretary of the U.S.A. Embassy, had been looted and one of the servants on the place killed. Today at noon I inspected the place, which is at 29 Ma Tai Chieh, and found it as stated. The house was in utter confusion, and the corpse of the servant was in one of the servants' rooms. The other servants had fled, so there is no one on the place now.

67. On December 19, Lee Wen Yuen, my chauffeur, living at 16 Lu Chia Lu (a German residence displaying the German flag and seals) together with his family of eight, was robbed by Japanese soldiers at 8:30 this morning of absolutely everything he possessed: seven boxes of clothing, two baskets of household things, six quilts, three mosquito nets, rice bowls and

dishes, and $50.00 in cash. The family is now destitute without even bed-covers.

69. On December 19 Meng Chai To, Chief Sanitary Inspector of our 8th Section, had the house where he is living at 59 Peiping Road entered six times yesterday and seven times today by Japanese soldiers. On the 17th two girls were raped there and again today two more were raped, one of them so brutally that she may die. Another girl was taken away from the place today. The refugees living in this house have been robbed of most of their money, watches, and other small articles.

72. On December 19 at the Rural Leaders' Training School, part of the University of Nanking, Japanese soldiers took $10.00 from one of our workers after having taken $2.50 from him the day before. During the afternoon two women were raped and during the night five more women were raped on the premises by Japanese soldiers.

73. On December 19 about 3 p.m. one Japanese soldier entered the University Hospital Compound and when Dr. McCallum and Dr. Trimmer, Superintendent, asked him to leave, the soldier fired his rifle at them. Fortunately, the shot passed to one side of Mr. McCallum.

75. On the evening of December 19, about 4:45 p.m. Dr. Bates was called to the house at 16 Ping Tsang Hsiang where Japanese soldiers had a few days previously driven out refugees. (Viewed by Riggs, Smith and Steele.) They had just finished looting the place and started a fire on the third floor. Dr. Bates tried to put out the fire but it was too late and the whole house burned to the ground.

76. On December 19, about 6 p.m. in the dark, six Japanese soldiers scaled the garden wall of Mr. Rabe's compound at Siao Tao Yuen. When he pointed his flashlight on one of them, he laid hand on his pistol but he soon realized that it would be bad business to shoot a German subject. Mr. Rabe ordered all six of them to go over the top of the wall back to where they came from. They tried to make him open the door for them but he strictly refused to do them the honor of passing

out of the door because they had come in without his permission.

77. On December 19, about 6 p.m., Dr. Bates, Mr. Fitch and Dr. Smythe were called to a University of Nanking house at 19 Hankow Road where a University staff man was living, in order to escort out four Japanese soldiers who were raping the women there. They found the soldiers in the basement where the women had been hidden. After sending the soldiers out over the wall all the women and children were escorted to the University of Nanking main buildings, where there was to be one Japanese Consular guard that night.

78. On the morning of December 20 about 7:30 when Mr. Riggs came by 28 Hankow Road he was called in and told that Japanese soldiers came during the night and because the women had been sent to the University of Nanking, the soldiers shot one man, stabbed another man seriously and three more or less seriously.

80. On December 20 about 7 a.m. Mr. McCallum, on his way home from standing guard at the University Hospital for the night, found many women and children on the way to the University for safety. Three families from different places told him that they had been burned out during the night by Japanese soldiers.

81. On December 20, about 3 a.m. two Japanese soldiers got into building No. 500 at Ginling Women's College and raped two women, even though a Japanese Consular policeman was at the gate on guard.

90. December 20. Today a blind barber came into the University Hospital. He was carrying his child on the 13th in the South City, when the Japanese soldiers came and asked him for money, and he had none so they shot him through the chest.

91. On December 20, a man who was the owner of a hat store in South City was shot in the chest when Japanese soldiers asked him for money and he gave them all he had. They asked for more and he could not produce it. He came to the University Hospital on the 20th.

92. On December 20, Japanese soldiers came into the Red Swastika Soup Kitchen at the University of Nanking, and took $7.00 from the accountant.

96. On December 20, five faculty residences clearly marked with an American flag and with the proclamations of the American Embassy were entered and looted. One of these houses has been entered again and again and three doors have been smashed in.

98. On December 20, at 7:30 p.m., a seventeen-year-old married girl, nine months pregnant, was raped by two Japanese soldiers; at 9:00 p.m. labor pains began; baby was born at 12:00 p.m. She was brought to the University Hospital this morning, because they could not get through the streets at night. Mother is hysterical but baby is doing well.

99. On December 20, afternoon, Japanese soldiers entered 5 Hankow Road, the house of Dr. J. H. Daniels, Superintendent of the University Hospital, with a Japanese proclamation on the front gate. They broke into the room upstairs, took two women into the house and raped them and spent three hours in the house. They took three bicycles from the cellar. Dr. Wilson has been using this house in the absence of Dr. Daniels.

101. On December 20, 3 p.m. three Japanese officers went into the office of the Refugee camp in the Hankow Road Primary School. The staff talked to them with an interpreter, but the officers ordered them out of the office and in broad daylight and in the same office raped two women.

102. On December 20, in the house of Mr. Schultze-Pantin (German), a member of the Committee, where Rev. Magee is living with Mr. Podshivoloff who is trying to help start the electric light plant and with Mr. Zial who is repairing cars at the Japanese Embassy, Japanese soldiers broke in and raped some of the women in front of the Chinese friends staying with Rev. Magee. (These people are good Christian families from the American Church Mission in Hsiakwan. They were aghast that any man could act in this way!)

100. On December 21, 1:15 p.m., Dr. Wilson found a soldier in the University Girls' Dormitory. He asked the soldier to leave and he threatened him with his pistol. Then, later, as Dr. Wilson passed the soldier on the road, the soldier loaded his rifle but did not fire.

105. On December 21. This afternoon Headquarters has about one hundred more women living in this immediate neighborhood who have been raped since last night and have come to the place for protection. (Women that came before have been sent to the University of Nanking.)

151. On December 22, two Japanese soldiers raped a refugee girl, aged thirteen, at the University of Nanking Sericulture Building and her mother was hurt when she tried to stop them. Another woman of twenty-eight years was also raped. On the 23rd, 4 a.m., two girls were taken by Japanese soldiers, but Japanese gendarmes met them and the Japanese soldiers fled.

146. On December 23, 3 p.m. two Japanese soldiers came to the Hankow Road Primary School Refugee Camp, searching for property and then raped a Miss Hwang of the staff. It was immediately reported to the Japanese Special Service Military Police. They sent Military Police to get the soldiers who had left, so they took the girl to their office and held her as witness. The same evening, other Japanese soldiers came and raped Mrs. Wang's daughter. About 7 p.m. three other Japanese soldiers raped two young girls, one of whom was only thirteen years old.

148. On December 25 night, seven Japanese soldiers came to the Bible Teachers' Training School Refugee Camp and stayed all night. During the day at 9 o'clock four soldiers came and at 2 o'clock three soldiers came and took clothing and money. They raped two women, one only twelve years old.

149. On December 25, 10 a.m. Mr. Riggs of the Committee was stopped on Hankow Road by an officer of the Inspection Corps who grabbed, hit and slapped Mr. Riggs.

This case was reported in detail in the following letter:

> 3 P'ing Ts'ang Hsiang,
> Nanking,
> December 25, 1937.

(Case 149)
To The Officers of the Imperial Japanese Embassy Nanking.

DEAR SIRS:

This morning about 10, Mr. Riggs found several soldiers in the house at No. 29 Hankow Road and heard a woman cry. The woman, who was about 25—30 years old, tapped herself and motioned for Mr. Riggs to come. One soldier had her in tow. Other soldiers were in the house. She grabbed Riggs' arm. The other soldiers came out of the house and all of them went on and left the woman with Mr. Riggs. She had been out to buy things and the soldiers took her. Her husband was taken four days ago and had not come back. She wanted Mr. Riggs to escort her back to the Refugee Camp at the Military College on Hankow Road. So Mr. Riggs escorted her east on Hankow Road and almost to the University Gardens and there they met an inspection officer with two soldiers and an interpreter.

The officer grabbed Mr. Riggs' hands out of his pockets and grabbed his armband, which had been issued him by the Japanese Embassy. He swatted Mr. Riggs' hands when he put them back in his pocket. As near as he could tell, the officer asked Riggs who he was, but neither could understand the other. He then hit Mr. Riggs on the chest hard. Mr. Riggs asked him what he meant and that made the officer angry. The officer motioned for his passport but Mr. Riggs did not have it with him. He wanted to know what Riggs was doing. Mr. Riggs told him he was taking this woman home. So the officer hit Mr. Riggs again. Mr. Riggs looked to see what armband the officer was wearing and the officer slapped Mr. Riggs in the face hard. The officer then pointed to the ground and grabbed Mr. Riggs' hat so Mr. Riggs thought the officer wanted him to kowtow to him. But Mr. Riggs would not. So the officer gave Mr. Riggs another slap in the face. Then the interpreter explained that the officer wanted a card.

Mr. Riggs explained he was taking the woman home because she was afraid. The officer gave an order to the soldiers and they came to either side of Mr. Riggs with guns at attention. Then the interpreter explained that the officer wanted Mr. Riggs to bow to him. Mr. Riggs refused because he was an American. The officer finally told Mr. Riggs to go home.

Meanwhile, the woman had been so frightened when she saw Mr. Riggs so treated, she ran on down Hankow Road.

Mr. Riggs explained that he did not touch the officer and simply had his hands in his pockets (of his overcoat) walking down the road bothering no one. The woman was walking a short distance ahead of him.

We hope that there will speedily be such a restoration of order and discipline among the soldiers that foreign nationals going peacefully about the streets need no longer fear being molested.

Most respectfullly yours,
(Signed) LEWIS S. C. SMYTHE.

152. On December 25, several Japanese soldiers took away the wheels of two large-type fire pump engines at 3 p.m. The Safety Zone Fire Department had four fire engines (cars) and twelve pumps. But in the last ten days nearly all have been taken by the Japanese soldiers. The pumps we have now are either destroyed or without wheels. Only one pump is usable.

154. On December 26, 4 p.m. a thirteen-year-old girl was raped by three Japanese soldiers at Chen Chia Shiai No. 6.

167. On December 27, 1 p.m. five Japanese soldiers and one servant came to Hankow Road Primary School and took away two girls. Fortunately, while these two girls were being dragged out, some Military Police came to our place for in-

spection and so they found this happening and captured the three soldiers and one servant.

169. On December 30, afternoon, two Japanese soldiers came to the residence of an official in the Italian Embassy, No. 64 Peiping Road, and took away more than $100.00 and two girls. After our earnest request, they released one girl but they still took away the other girl, named Hsan Shi-tse, age sixteen, wearing fur-lined clothes. Three Japanese soldiers went in while two watched at the gate.

APPENDIX B

CASE REPORTS COVERING CHAPTER V

THE CASES GIVEN *below were filed with the Japanese authorities during the period from January 1 to January 12 covered by the two letters reproduced in Appendix D (Z 27 and BZ 33)*:

Case No.

171. *Jan.* 1, 1938. 3 p.m. Mr. Sperling was walking along Ninghai Road near the corner of Kwangchow Road and an old woman came running out of a house. Mr. Sperling went in and one Japanese soldier ran away but in a bedroom Mr. Sperling found a Japanese soldier completely undressed and a Chinese girl he had just finished raping partly undressed. Mr. Sperling told him to get out but gave him time to get his clothes on.

172. *Jan.* 1, 9 p.m. Japanese soldiers came with a truck to Mr. Rabe's house, Siao Tao Yuen, and asked for a truck load of girls. Mr. Rabe refused them entrance so they went on to the University Middle School.

173. *Jan.* 1, in the afternoon three Japanese soldiers went inside the Ginling College Campus. One followed a girl into a garden where there are many bamboo trees. Miss Vautrin was called and saved the girl just in time from being raped. Miss Vautrin saw the other two Japanese soldiers who claimed they were Military Police.

174. *Jan.* 1, at 1:40 p.m. two Japanese soldiers entered the house in which Rev. Forster is living at 17 Lo Kai Lu and raped one girl, and beat up another who resisted their attempt to rape her. Rev. Forster was out to dinner with Mr. Fitch. Messrs. Fitch, Magee and Forster rushed to the place in a car and took the two girls to the University Hospital for treatment.

175. *Jan.* 1, at 4 p.m. in a University house (American property) at 11 Hankow Road, three Japanese soldiers raped a fourteen-year-old girl. A woman in the house went to the University gate for Military Police but they came slowly and were too late.

176. One Japanese soldier came between 10 and 11 a.m. on January 2, 1938, to the house where Liu Pan-kwen and his wife and five children were living, Ch'en Chia Hsiang No. 5. This soldier tried to investigate the house. Then he saw this woman, the wife of Liu Pan-kwen, and asked questions about the condition of the house. The woman began to answer these questions. Those who stayed in the house saw this so they hinted to the woman to leave the house because the soldier was trying to get the woman into a room. So the woman was trying to leave. At the same time her husband, Liu Pan-kwen, said some rough words to the soldiers and also slapped his face. Then the soldier left. The woman came back and started to cook rice, and her husband was trying to bring the food to eat with his five children. The soldier came back with a gun about 4 p.m. This Japanese soldier asked for the husband and the neighbors pled with him for the man's life and one man even knelt down before the Japanese soldier. The husband was hiding in the kitchen. As soon as the Japanese soldier caught sight of him, he shot him instantly through the shoulder. Dr. H. was called about 4:30 p.m. and found the man dead. Rev. John Magee came a little later and found the same situation.

178. *Jan.* 3, a woman who was taken with 5 others from No. 6 Chien Ying Hsiang ostensibly for washing clothes for Japanese officers, on December 30 came to the University Hospital. She stated that they were taken by Japanese soldiers to a house in the west central portion of the city which she thought must be a Japanese military hospital. The women washed clothes during the day and were raped throughout the night. The older ones being raped from ten to twenty times; the younger and good-looking ones as many as forty times a night. On January 2, two soldiers took our patient with them to a deserted school house and struck her ten times with a bayonet knife; four times

APPENDIX B

on the back of the neck severing the muscles down to the vertebral column; once on wrist, once on the face, and four on the back. She will probably recover but will have a stiff neck. The soldiers left her for dead. She was found by another Japanese soldier who saw her condition and took her to some friends who brought her to the Hospital. (Actually she died of meningitis.)

179. *Jan. 3*, a fourteen-year-old girl, physically immature, was raped with disastrous results that will require considerable surgical repair.

182. *On Jan. 7* two Japanese soldiers wanted to rape a young girl. Chang Foh-hsi tried to prevent them and was stabbed at Tze Pei Hsie, No. 7.

180. *On Jan. 8* five or six Japanese soldiers after raping shot at the inmates of No. 22 Shen Chu Ren Hsiang, wounding a woman named Lee, aged thirty-two.

181. *On Jan. 8* four Japanese soldiers broke into a house of the Yuan family, at No. 45 Kao Kyia Chiu Kwang, at night and raped three women (aged 21, 25, 29). When they were slow in complying with their desires they shot at them with a pistol.

183. *On Jan. 8, 6 p.m.* three Japanese pilots raped a girl, eighteen years old, named Kao at No. 4 Kwa Chiao Road and shot at random with pistols.

184. *On Jan. 9* an old man returned to Taikoo Shan from the Safety Zone to see about his home and if he could move back. When he got there, three Japanese soldiers were at the door and without a word one of the soldiers shot the old man through both legs. He is now at the University Hospital.

185. *On the morning of Jan. 9*, Mr. Kroeger and Mr. Hatz saw a Japanese officer and soldier executing a poor man in civilian clothes in a pond inside the Safety Zone on Shansi Road, just east of the Sino-British Boxer Indemnity Building. The man was standing in the pond up to his waist in water on which the ice was broken and was wobbling around when Mr. Kroeger and Hatz arrived. The officer gave an order and the soldier lay down behind a sandbag and fired a rifle at the man and hit

him in one shoulder. He fired again and missed the man. The third shot killed him.[1]

186. *On Jan.* 9 about 3 p.m. Rev. Mills and Dr. Smythe went to Shuan Tang to see about conditions there with a view to learning how the situation was for people to return to that part of the southwest portion of the city. When they got there they found that a woman with a baby in her arms had just been raped by three Japanese soldiers.

187. *On the night of Jan* 9, a military policeman took a woman from Dr. Smythe's house at No. 25 Hankow Road and another from another house. He met Mr. Riggs returning to his home at No. 23 Hankow Road, and threatened him with a bayonet.

188. *Jan.* 12, this morning two men (Ma and Ying) who have been registered[2] returned to the home of Ma at Hansimen to see about Ma's blind mother whom a neighbor said Japanese soldiers had killed. They found the body of Ma's mother. On the way back the two men met Japanese soldiers who demanded their clothes, then stabbed them and carried the two bodies into a dugout. One of them came to and crawled out. People saw him and gave him clothes. Then he walked back to the Sericulture Building. Two friends carried him on a bed to our Headquarters. Mr. Fitch sent him with them to the University Hospital.

[1] We have no right to protest about legitimate executions by the Japanese Army, but this certainly was carried out in an inefficient and brutal way. Furthermore, it brings up a matter we have mentioned many times in private conversation with the Japanese Embassy men: this killing of people in ponds within the Zone has spoiled and thereby seriously curtailed the reserve water supply for the people in the Zone. This is very serious in this long dry spell and with the city water coming so slowly. [Note by reporter.]

[2] See Chapter III.

APPENDIX C

CASE REPORTS COVERING PERIOD JANUARY 14, 1938, TO FEBRUARY 9, 1938

THE FOLLOWING SELECTION *of cases reported to the Japanese authorities covers the period from January 14 to February 9 and so completes the story of the first two months of the Japanese Army's occupation of Nanking. A total of 444 cases were written up but many of the earlier ones were compound cases involving many people. Beginning with case 190 these cases show the difficulties Chinese families met in trying to return to their homes outside the Zone. The order for such return was given by the Japanese on the afternoon of January 28.*

Case No.
219. Mr. John Magee has an account of a family in South City of thirteen in which eleven were killed, women raped and mutilated, on December 13-14 by Japanese soldiers. Two small children survived to tell the story.
190. Jan. 14, a family went home from the University Middle School. On the way they got their new registration paper which they were told to paste on their door and they would not be troubled by soldiers. They did this and within an hour three Japanese soldiers came in and forced out the men and raped the women five times. So on Jan. 15 they came back to the Middle School to live.
195. Jan. 17, a woman from a family in the University Middle School went home with a man of the same family. Their home is in the newly-opened southern section of the city. A Japanese soldier came in and insisted on sleeping with her. She refused and the soldier killed her with a bayonet.
198. Jan. 19, a Buddhist nun living at present in the same house with Forster and myself reports that yesterday she got word

that her uncle, a man of sixty-five years by the name of Chu had gone to buy rice in one of the places designated by the Japanese, had first been robbed by Japanese soldiers on the road and then stabbed to death. This had happened about a week before as her uncle had gone to buy the rice but had not returned and they did not know what had happened to him.

199. Jan. 20, Mr. Magee reports that the wounded Chinese soldiers in the Red Cross Hospital at the Ministry of Foreign Affairs are only fed three bowls of rice per day. One man complained to a Japanese officer (or doctor?). The officer slapped him and then when the man further objected, he was taken out and bayoneted.

211. Jan. 25, afternoon, a Chinese woman came to the University Hospital. She and her husband had moved into the Safety Zone and were living in a straw hut near the Bible Teachers' Training School. On December 13 her husband was taken away by the Japanese soldiers and the wife, this woman, was taken to South City where she has been ever since. She has been raped every day from seven to ten times since but usually was given an opportunity to sleep at night. She has developed all three types of venereal disease in their most virulent forms: Syphilis, Gonorrhea, Chancroid. She was let go five days ago probably because of her diseased condition. She returned to the Zone then.

215. Jan. 28, 9:00 p.m. Japanese soldiers came into the T'ien Min Bath House at T'u Chieh K'o on Chung Shan Tung Lu (east of the Special Service Corps office and in the area assigned to soldiers), searched the workers for money and shot three of them. Two of the workers were wounded and one killed. This bathhouse was opened by the Self-Government Committee at the request of the Japanese and was supposed to have their special protection.

230. Jan. 29, a woman returned, aged twenty-two. Her husband was bayoneted by Japanese soldiers and died several days before. When she herself returned home to No. 2 Shan Pei Lu on Jan. 29, she was raped by Japanese soldiers three times.

APPENDIX C

232. Jan. 29, Chen Wang Shih, twenty-eight, returned home. On the road she and another woman were stopped by three soldiers, who asked them to follow. Despite pleadings on their knees, they were pulled into a shop. Mrs. Chen was raped three times.

337. Jan. 29, Mr. Yao returned to Chan Fu Yuan, his home, in the afternoon. Some Japanese soldiers robbed cases of matches from them that day. On the 30th some Japanese went there and stripped off the clothes from all members of his family, including an eighty-year-old woman, to find if they had money. But they had none. At the same time Mr. Zee of the next door was robbed of $3.50. On Feb. 1 there came three Japanese soldiers searching in the same way. They intend to return to camp.

353. Jan. 29, Hwang Cheh Shih, at Tsai Er Hsiang, aged thirty-nine, was raped by Japanese soldiers over 10 times by turn.

222. Jan. 30, a family moved home from the Sericulture Building into a house at 30-25 Er Tiao Hsiang because of the order to leave the camps. That night three Japanese soldiers broke down the fence in the back, came around the house and knocked on the front door. Not being admitted they pounded the door in, turned on the light, ordered the man to get up. Then explained that they were "detectives." One man carried a sword, one a rifle, and the third was without arms. They explained very carefully that the people need not be afraid and they would not do any harm to them and for the man to lie down again and go to sleep, which he did. They searched the place for money and then the man with the sword raped a twelve-year-old girl and the other two raped an old woman. The soldiers left about midnight. So the family moved back to camp on the 31st.

224. Jan. 30, about 5 p.m. Mr. Sone was greeted by several hundred women pleading with him that they would not have to go home on February 4. They said it was no use going home they might just as well be killed for staying at the camp as to be raped, robbed or killed at home. They said, "You have saved us half-way, if you let us go now what use is there unless

you save us the other half?" One old woman, sixty-two years, went home near Hansimen and soldiers came at night and wanted to rape her. She said she was too old. So the soldiers rammed a stick up her. But she survived to come back.

290. Jan. 30, 11 a.m. No. 19 Huang Li Hsiang Chao Tien Kung, a girl refugee of Ginling College went home to pay a visit. Suddenly there came four soldiers who raped this young girl a little over ten years of age by turn.

378. Jan. 30, Mrs. Chen went home and while she was walking on the street of Shih San Chieh, she met three Japanese soldiers who pulled her to Hen Mao Gian Yuan (a shop) and raped her by turn. When rape was finished, she was released. (Chopped by her right hand second finger.)

333. Jan. 31, at 8 p.m. two soldiers came to the home of an old woman, seventy-one years old, who lives at Mo Fan Ive, in the San Pei Lou district. They crawled to the top of her hut evidently to listen whether there were any girls inside. When the old woman heard the noise on the roof she came out and they came down. They went in and asked for girls but she said there were none, whereupon they beat her. They tried to take off her trousers but she resisted. So they hit her over the head with something they had picked up in the house.

223. Feb. 1. This morning at 6:30 a group of women gathered a second time to greet Dr. Bates when he left the University. They told him they could not go home. Among other cases one woman who feared that she would lose her bedding when the camp was sealed, took her two daughters home yesterday, to Hsi Hwa Men. Last evening Japanese soldiers came and demanded to have a chance to rape the girls. The two girls objected and the soldiers bayoneted them to death. The woman says there is no use going home. If they are going to be killed at home they might just as well be killed at the camp by soldiers attempting to drive them out.

327. Feb. 1, at 1 p.m. three Japanese soldiers came to Wu Tiao Hsiang, Drum Tower, and carried off a girl of little over ten years of age. The same family had been visited by three Japanese soldiers on Jan. 28, who raped two women.

APPENDIX C 165

382. Feb. 1, Wu Chang-seng returned to his home at Kwang Hwa Men (outside) and after arriving seven Japanese soldiers there brought on old woman and ordered them to make sexual connection together. The Japanese soldiers laughed by the side.
375. Feb. 3, Mrs. Ma returned home and while she was walking in front of a house on Tung Ren Chieh, she met three Japanese soldiers who dragged her to an empty house and then raped her by turn. (Chopped by her right hand 2nd finger.)
442. Feb. 2, a family was carrying vegetables into the city and was stopped by some Japanese soldiers near Chunghwamen. They forced the man to kneel in the road and asked him for "hua Ku-niang." They told him to throw away his vegetables and the man demurred whereupon the soldier took the butt of his rifle and drove it down on the man's lower leg, breaking both bones. It took him two days to get to the hospital.
426. Feb. 5. Tsao Tsen Shih lives at No. 56 Hansimen. On the forenoon one Japanese soldier came into her house and attempted to rape her. But others in the house called the Military Police. The soldier came again at 5 p.m. and used a bayonet to wound her face. She was sent to the University Hospital to have her wounds dressed. Dr. Wilson who is attending the case, says that the wounds on her face are very serious and since the woman was semi-unconscious he feared the skull had been fractured.
430. Feb. 5, a Japanese soldier came to the house of Mr. Chen at Te Chung Bridge, near Hsi Hwa Gate, and asked for a girl. As there was no girl he pulled away a young man of about seventeen or eighteen years old and committed sodomy. Obeying the original instructions, the family had sent the older men back home.
436. Feb. 5. An old woman named Chen, over sixty, at San Pai Lou, was visited by three Japanese soldiers. One was stationed outside while the other two raped the old woman by turn. One of the soldiers asked her to clean the penis by her mouth. Her grandson was stabbed twice for crying.
444. Feb. 6. The man reporting this had been taken by the Japanese and worked for them for a month outside Chung Shan

Men. They gave him three yen as a month's wages. They sent him back because that detachment left for other parts. A few days later he and some friends were taking some empty burlap sacks from Ninghai Road along Kwangchow Road. A soldier on a hilltop stopped them and motioned them to return. They turned around and had gone about forty steps when a shot from behind shattered this man's left arm below the elbow so severely that it had to be amputated. He has three dependents, was shot on the 6th. (Wilson)

428. Feb. 7, a twelve-year-old girl was raped at midnight. Her parents had just moved home to Ta Fang Hsiang the day before. Her father returned the girl to the camp. She has suffered so much that even now she cannot walk and the injured part of her body was swelled, according to her father.

APPENDIX D

CORRESPONDENCE BETWEEN SAFETY ZONE COMMITTEE AND JAPANESE AUTHORITIES, ETC.

THE INTERNATIONAL COMMITTEE *for the Nanking Safety Zone had received full recognition from the Chinese authorities but from the Japanese only a statement that they would not intentionally attack the area if there were no Chinese military forces in it.*

The Chinese authorities had been slow in withdrawing non-active military establishments, had failed to remove a small anti-aircraft gun installed inside the south-west boundary of the Zone, and Chinese forces retreated through the Zone on the night of December 12. But by the morning of the 13th they were out, so there was no actual contact between the two armies in the Zone. (Japanese artillery had made nine hits in the southern part of the Zone, killing about forty people.) The promoters thus hoped that, at least after the first few days of chaos resulting from the Chinese withdrawal and the Japanese occupation, normality would return of itself, even if business and cultivation could not revive at once, and the refugees would, with assistance, be able to go back to their homes and assume a semblance of ordinary existence.

The Committee approached the Japanese forces with as little delay as possible. The Chairman made contact with the Japanese advance guard on Han Chung Road on the afternoon of December 13 and tried to explain the Zone to him. The Zone was not marked on his map. On the morning of December 14 the Committee tried to present to the officer in command the following letter (Doc. No. 1) but were referred to the Chief of the T'eh Wu Chi Kwan (Special Service Organ or "Corps") who would not arrive until the next day. The latter granted the Chairman an interview at noon on December 15, after which General Harada inspected the Zone and paid a visit to the Zone Headquarters.

168   JAPANESE TERROR IN CHINA

DOCUMENT No. 1 (Z 1)
INTERNATIONAL COMMITTEE FOR NANKING SAFETY ZONE
5, Ninghai Road
December 14, 1937

Japanese Commander of Nanking.
HONORABLE SIR:

We come to thank you for the fine way your artillery spared the Safety Zone and to establish contact with you for future plans for care of Chinese civilians in the Zone.

The International Committee has taken responsibility for putting people into buildings in the area, has stored rice and flour for feeding the population temporarily, and has taken control of the police in the area.

We would respectfully request that the Committee may:

1. Be favored with a Japanese guard at entrances to the Safety Zone.
2. Be allowed to police the inside of the area with its own civilian police who are armed only with pistols.
3. Be allowed to carry on sale of rice and operate its soup kitchens in the area.
    a. We have stores of rice in other parts of the city and would like to have free passage of trucks to secure them.
4. Be allowed to continue the present housing arrangements until the common people can return to their homes. (Even then there will be thousands of homeless poor refugees to care for.)
5. Be given the opportunity to cooperate with you in restoring telephone, electric, and water services as soon as possible.

Yesterday afternoon an unforeseen situation developed when a number of Chinese soldiers were trapped in the northern part of the city. Some of them came to our office and pleaded in the name of humanity that we save their lives. Representatives of our Committee tried to find your Headquarters but got no farther than a captain on Han Chung Lu. So we disarmed all these soldiers and put them into buildings in the Zone. We beg your merciful permission to return these men to peaceful civilian life as is now their desire.

We would further like to introduce to you the "International Red Cross Committee of Nanking" with Rev. John Magee (Ameri-

APPENDIX D 169

can) as Chairman. This International Red Cross Committee has taken charge of the former military hospitals at the Ministry of Foreign Affairs, the Ministry of Railways, and the Ministry of War, the Red Cross Committee yesterday disarmed all men on these places and will see that these buildings are used only for hospital purposes. If it is possible to put all the wounded in it, we suggest transferring all the Chinese wounded to the Ministry of Foreign Affairs building.

We will be glad to cooperate in any way we can in caring for the civilian population of this city.

Most respectfully yours,
INTERNATIONAL COMMITTEE FOR NANKING
SAFETY ZONE
John H. D. Rabe, Chairman.

INTERNATIONAL COMMITTEE FOR NANKING SAFETY ZONE
5, Ninghai Road.
Telephones: 31961
32346
31641

Membership List

Name	Nationality	Organization
1. Mr. John H. D. Rabe, Chairman	German	Siemens Co.
2. Dr. Lewis S. C. Smythe, Secretary	American	University of Nanking
3. Mr. P. H. Munro-Faure	British	Asiatic Petroleum Co.
4. Rev. John Magee	American	American Church Mission
5. Mr. P. R. Shields	British	International Export Co.
6. Mr. J. M. Hanson	Danish	Texas Oil Co.
7. Mr. G. Schultze-Pantin	German	Shingming Trading Co.
8. Mr. Ivor Mackay	British	Butterfield and Swire
9. Mr. J. V. Pickering	American	Standard-Vacuum Oil Co.

Membership List (Continued)

Name	Nationality	Organization
10. Mr. Eduard Sperling	German	Shanghai Insurance Office
11. Dr. M. S. Bates	American	University of Nanking
12. Rev. W. P. Mills	American	Northern Presbyterian Mission
13. Mr. J. Lean	British	Asiatic Petroleum Co.
14. Dr. C. S. Trimmer	American	University Hospital
15. Mr. Charles Riggs	American	University of Nanking

INTERNATIONAL RED CROSS COMMITTEE OF NANKING
5, Ninghai Road.
Telephones: 32346
31641
31961

1. Rev. John C. Magee, Chairman
2. Mr. Li Chuin-nan, Vice-Chairman
   (Chinese Red Cross Society of Nanking)
3. Mr. W. Lowe, Vice-Chairman
4. Rev. Ernest H. Forster, Secretary
5. Mr. Christian Kroeger, Treasurer
6. Mrs. Paul de Witt Twinem
7. Miss Minnie Vautrin
8. Dr. Robert O. Wilson
9. Mr. P. H. Munro-Faure
10. Dr. C. S. Trimmer
11. Rev. James McCallum
12. Dr. M. S. Bates
13. Mr. John H. D. Rabe
14. Dr. Lewis S. C. Smythe
15. Rev. W. P. Mills
16. Mr. Cola Podshivoloff
17. Pastor Shen Yu-shu

Since contact could not be established with the Japanese Commander on December 14 and several groups of disarmed Chinese soldiers and civilians were tied up and marched off on that day in spite of the protests by the members of the Committee, the Committee decided that a more comprehensive statement regarding disarmed Chinese soldiers in the Zone should be made. So on the morning of December 15 the Chairman of the Committee addressed a letter to the Attaché at the Japanese Embassy (now Vice-Consul) as follows (Doc. No. 2). This letter was presented to Mr. Fukuda at the same time as Document No. 1 during the forenoon of December 15. He had come to the Zone Headquarters to inquire about the Zone. Consequently, the statement by the Chief of the Special Service Corps at noon that day was also an answer to this letter. (See Document No. 4.)

DOCUMENT No. 2 (Z 4)
INTERNATIONAL COMMITTEE FOR NANKING SAFETY ZONE
5, Ninghai Road
December 15, 1937.

Mr. Tokuyasu Fukuda,
Attaché to the Japanese Embassy,
Nanking.

DEAR SIR:

The International Committee for Nanking Safety Zone is very much perplexed by the problem of soldiers who have thrown away their arms. From the beginning the Committee strove to have this Zone entirely free of Chinese soldiers and up to the afternoon of Monday, December 13, had achieved considerable success in this respect. At that time several hundred soldiers approached or entered the Zone through the northern boundary and appealed to us for help. The Committee plainly told the soldiers that it could not protect them. But we told them that if they abandoned their arms and all resistance to the Japanese, we thought the Japanese would give them merciful treatment.

In the confusion and haste of that evening, the Committee was unable to keep the disarmed soldiers separate from civilians, particularly because some of the soldiers had abandoned their military clothing.

The Committee fully recognizes that identified soldiers are lawful prisoners of war. But in dealing with these disarmed soldiers, the Committee hopes that the Japanese Army will use every precaution not to involve civilians. The Committee further hopes that the Japanese Army will in accordance with the recognized laws of war regarding prisoners and for reasons of humanity exercise mercy toward these former soldiers. They might be used to good advantage as laborers and would be glad to return to civilian life if possible.

Most respectfully yours,
JOHN D. RABE.
John H. D. Rabe, Chairman.

At the same time the International Red Cross Society asked the Attaché's assistance for their Society from the Japanese Military Authorities:

DOCUMENT No. 3 (Z 5)
INTERNATIONAL RED CROSS SOCIETY, NANKING BRANCH
5, Ninghai Road
December 15, 1937.

Tokuyasu Fukuda, Esquire,
Attaché to the Japanese Embassy,
Nanking.

SIR:

Owing to the large number of wounded soldiers and civilians in Nanking, we have organized a local branch of the International Red Cross Society to deal with the situation.

We have appealed for recognition from the International Red Cross Society in Shanghai and from the Red Cross Society of China.

We now request your good offices in securing for us permission from the Japanese Military Authorities in Nanking to carry on this humanitarian work.

We herewith enclose a list[1] of the membership of our Committee. With kind regards, I am,

Yours cordially,
ERNEST H. FORSTER,
Secretary.

[1] See list submitted with Document No. 1.

APPENDIX D

The brief interview was granted by the Chief of the Japanese Special Service Corps to the Safety Zone Committee. This interview was merely a statement made by way of reply to the Committee's letter of December 14 (See Document No. 1 [Z 1]). Point 9 refers to rice the Committee had not been able to haul in the Zone before the entry of the Japanese troops. A rough minute of the interview follows:

DOCUMENT No. 4 (Z 6)
MEMORANDUM OF INTERVIEW WITH CHIEF OF SPECIAL SERVICE CORPS

Bank of Communications, noon, December 15, 1937.

Translator: Mr. Fukuda. (The interview was a categorical statement by the Chief and no questions or discussion. It was in answer to our letter of December 14th, which had been given to Mr. Fukuda that morning and was presented to the Chief in Japanese.)

1. Must search the city for Chinese soldiers.
2. Will post guards at entrances to Zone.
3. People should return to their homes as soon as possible, therefore, we must search the Zone.
4. Trust humanitarian attitude of Japanese Army to care for the disarmed Chinese soldiers.
5. Police may patrol within the Zone if they are disarmed excepting for batons.
6. The ten thousand *tan* of rice stored by your Committee in the Zone you may use for the refugees. But Japanese soldiers need rice so in the Zone they should be allowed to buy rice. (Answer regarding our stores of rice outside of Zone not clear.)
7. Telephone, electricity, and water must be repaired, so this P.M. will go with Mr. Rabe to inspect and act accordingly.
8. We are anxious to get workers. From tomorrow will begin to clear city. Committee please assist. Will pay. Tomorrow want one hundred to two hundred workers.
9. Will inspect rice locations and guard.

(Signed) LEWIS S. C. SMYTHE,
Secretary, International Committee for Nanking Safety Zone.

Members of Committee present:
Mr. Rabe, Chairman
Dr. Smythe, Sec.
Mr. Sperling, Inspector-General.

On the 16th the Committee addressed to the Japanese Attaché the first letter requesting the restoration of order and drawing attention to the growing savagery which was occurring in the city.

DOCUMENT No. 5 (Z 8)
INTERNATIONAL COMMITTEE FOR NANKING SAFETY ZONE
5, Ninghai Road
December 16, 1937.

Mr. Tokuyasu Fukuda,
Attaché to the Japanese Embassy,
Nanking.

MY DEAR SIR:

As pointed out by the Major we interviewed with you at the Bank of Communications yesterday noon, it is advisable to have the city return to normal life as soon as possible. But yesterday the continued disorders committed by Japanese soldiers in the Safety Zone increased the state of panic among the refugees. Refugees in large buildings are afraid to even go to nearby soup kitchens to secure the cooked rice. Consequently, we are having to deliver rice to these compounds directly, thereby complicating our problem. We could not even get coolies out to load rice and coal to take to our soup kitchens and therefore this morning thousands of people had to go without their breakfast. Foreign members of the International Committee are this morning making desperate efforts to get trucks through Japanese patrols so these civilians can be fed. Yesterday foreign members of our Committee had several attempts made to take their personal cars away from them by Japanese soldiers. (A list of cases of disorder is appended.)

Until this state of panic is allayed, it is going to be impossible to get any normal activity started in the city, such as: telephone workers, electric plant workers, probably the water plant workers, shops of all kinds, or even street cleaning.

In order to quickly improve this situation, the International Committee respectfully suggests that the Imperial Japanese Army take the following steps at once:

1. Have all searching done by regularly organized squads of soldiers under a responsible officer (Most of the trouble has come from wandering groups of three to seven soldiers without an officer.)

2. At night, and if possible also in the daytime, have the guards at the entrances of the Safety Zone (proposed by the Major yesterday) to prevent any stray Japanese soldiers from entering the Safety Zone.

3. Today, give us passes to paste on the windshields of our private cars and trucks to prevent Japanese soldiers from commandeering them. (Even under the stress of defense of the city the Chinese Army Headquarters supplied us with such passes and the cars that were taken before we got the passes were returned to the Committee within twenty-four hours after our reporting the cases. Furthermore, even in that difficult situation, the Chinese Army assigned to us three trucks to use for hauling rice for feeding civilians. Certainly, the Imperial Japanese Army in full control of the city, with no fighting going on, and with much greater amount of equipment, cannot do less for the Chinese civilians that have now come under their care and protection.)

We refrained from protesting yesterday because we thought when the High Command arrived order in the city would be restored, but last night was even worse than the night before, so we decided these matters should be called to the attention of the Imperial Japanese Army, which we are sure does not approve such actions by its soldiers.

Most respectfully yours,

(Signed) LEWIS S. C. SMYTHE,
Secretary.

John H. D. Rabe, Chairman.

At an interview on the afternoon of the 16th the Japanese Consul-General called on the Committee and informed them that they (the Japanese) had not recognized the Committee but would deal with them as though they had been recognized. Mr. Kiyoshi Fukui was introduced at that time as the man with whom the Committee should deal. So a letter was addressed to the Japanese Embassy on the 17th explaining the anomalous situation and seeking to come to some understanding with the Japanese that would facilitate the restoration of order among their troops in the city.

DOCUMENT No. 6 (Z 9)
INTERNATIONAL COMMITTEE FOR NANKING SAFETY ZONE
5, Ninghai Road
December 17, 1937.

The Imperial Japanese Embassy
Nanking.

For the kind attention of:
Mr. Kiyoshi Fukui,
Second Secretary to the Japanese Embassy.

DEAR SIRS:

In view of the statement of Consul-General Katsuo Okazaki yesterday afternoon that the International Committee had no legal status, some explanations of our position seem to be in order. *Vis-à-vis* your Japanese authorities we are not claiming any political status whatever. But on December 1st, Mayor Ma of the Nanking Municipality turned over to our Committee nearly all the functions of the City Government for the emergency of transitions: police, supervision of essential utilities, fire department, housing regulation, food supply, and sanitation. Consequently, when your Army victoriously arrived in the city on Monday noon, December 13, we were the only administrative authority carrying on in the city. Of course, that authority did not extend outside of the Safety Zone itself, and involved no rights of sovereignty within the Zone.

Being the only administrative authorities and having had assurances from the Japanese authorities in Shanghai that if the Safety Zone did not contain soldiers or military establishments, your troops would not intentionally attack it, we tried to establish contact with your advance guard immediately. In the afternoon of December 13, we found a captain with a group of Japanese soldiers resting on *Han Chung Lu*. We explained to him where the Zone was and marked it on his map. We politely called his attention to the three Red Cross Hospitals and told him about the disarmed soldiers. He was reassuring so we felt that all was understood by your Army.

That night and early the next morning we drew up our letter of December 14 and had it translated into Japanese. Then, as Mr. Fukuda, Attaché to the Imperial Japanese Embassy, may tell you, Mr. Rabe, Mr. Smythe, and Rev. Forster went to find a high Japanese officer to whom we could present the letter. We talked to five different officers but they told us to wait for the arrival of the High Commander the next day.

The following morning, December 15, we were favored by calls by Mr. Tokuyasu Fukuda of the Imperial Japanese Embassy, and by Mr. Sekiguchi with cards from the Captain and Officers of the H.I.J.M.S. "Seta" at our headquarters. We presented our letter of December 14, referred to above, to Mr. Fukuda, and assured Mr. Sekiguchi that we would be glad to cooperate in starting the electricity works. At noon, we had the pleasure of meeting the Head of the T'eh Pei Kwan Chang (Special Service) at the Bank of Communications and from him received a formal oral statement in answer to our letter of December 14. In his reply, among other points, he said that they would station guards at the entrance to the Zone; that the civilian police could patrol within the Zone provided they were armed only with batons; that the Committee could use the ten thousand *tan* of rice it had stored and move in the other stores of rice assigned to it by the former City Government; and that it was essential to repair the telephone, electricity and water works as soon as possible. But no answer was given to point 4 in our letter of the 14th excepting to say that people should return to their homes as soon as possible.

On the basis of this reply, we encouraged our police to go ahead with their duties, assured the people they would be well-treated now that we had explained to the Japanese officers, and started to move rice. But since then any truck that appeared on the streets without a Westerner on it has been commandeered; the Red Swastika Society (working under our direction), which started trucks Tuesday morning to pick up dead bodies in the Zone, had its trucks either taken or attempts made to take them and now yesterday fourteen of their workers were taken away. Our police were interfered with and yesterday fifty of them stationed at the Ministry of Justice were marched off, "to be killed" according to the Japanese officer in charge, and yesterday afternoon forty-six of our "volunteer police" were similarly marched off. (These volunteers had been organised by our Committee on December 13 when it looked as though the work to be done in the Zone was greater than the uniformed police—who were on day and night duty—could take care of. These "volunteer police" were neither uniformed nor armed in any way. They simply wore our armbands. They were more like Boy Scouts in the West who do odd jobs in helping to keep crowds in order, clean up, and render first aid, etc.) On the 14th our four fire trucks were commandeered by Japanese soldiers and used for transport.

The point we have been trying so hard to get across to your Embassy and to the Japanese Army is that we were left to carry on the City Government services for the civilian population of Nanking until the Japanese authorities could establish a new City Government or other organization to take over these functions in the city. But unfortunately your soldiers have not been willing to let us continue with our maintenance of order and services for the civilian population in the Zone. This resulted in a breaking down of our system for maintaining order and for providing necessary services which we had carried on up till the morning of December 14. In other words, on the 13th when your troops entered the city, we had nearly all the civilian population gathered in a Zone in which there had been very little destruction by stray shells and no looting by Chinese soldiers even when in full retreat. The stage was all set for you to take over that area peacefully and let the normal life therein continue undisturbed until the rest of the city could be put in order. Then the full normal life of the city could go forward. All twenty-seven Westerners in the city at that time and our Chinese population were totally surprised by the reign of robbery, rapine, and killing initiated by your soldiers on the 14th.

All that we are asking in our protests is that you restore order amongst your troops and get the normal life of the city going as soon as possible. In the latter process we are glad to cooperate in any way we can. But even last night between 8 and 9 p.m. when five Western members of our staff and Committee toured the Zone to observe conditions, we did not find a single Japanese patrol either in the Zone or at the entrances! Yesterday's threats and marching off of our police had driven all our police from the streets. All we saw were groups of two and three Japanese soldiers wandering about the streets of the Zone and now, as I write, reports are pouring in from all parts of the Zone about the depredations of robbery and rape committed by these wondering, uncontrolled soldiers. This means that nothing has been done about our requests in our letter of yesterday, December 16, namely point 2, that stray soldiers be kept out of the Zone by guards at the entrances.

Consequently, as a first step in turning over to your authorities the maintenance of order in the Zone, we suggest:

1. That the Imperial Japanese Army set up a system of regular military police to patrol the Zone both day and night with full authority to arrest soldiers found looting, entering houses, and committing rape or carrying off women.

2. That the Japanese authorities take over the 450 Chinese police assigned to us by the former Chinese Nanking City Government and organize them to maintain peace and order among the civilian population. (This order has *never* once broken down in the Zone.)

3. In view of the number of fires in the city yesterday and last night, fortunately not in the Zone, we suggest that the Fire Department be re-organized under your authorities and the four trucks be returned by your soldiers to such service.

4. We further respectfully beg to suggest that as soon as possible you kindly bring an expert in Municipal Administration to Nanking to manage the life of the civilian population until a new city government can be formed. (There is nothing left of the former city government excepting the police and firemen in our Zone and three clerks. All others left the city. Your army has taken the physical structure of the city of Nanking and the poorer sections of its population, but most of the trained, intelligent and active people have all moved further west.)

May we again reassure you that we have no interest in continuing any semi-administrative function left to us by the former Nanking City Government. We earnestly hope that you will kindly take up these functions as quickly as possible. Then we will become simply a relief organization.

If the depredations of the last three days continue, this relief problem is going to be multiplied rapidly. We organized the Zone on the basis that every family that could should make private arrangements for housing and food in order to reduce the administrative load suddenly placed on our *ad hoc* organization. But if the present situation continues, in a few days we are going to have large numbers of people facing starvation; their private supplies of food and fuel are running out; money, clothing, and personal articles have been taken from many of them by wandering Japanese soldiers; and little normal business or other activity can be carried on because people are afraid to either open shops or appear on the streets. On the other hand, since the morning of December 14, our supply trucks have been practically at a standstill. Before your troops entered the city we concentrated on getting supplies into the Zone and expected to carry out distribution later because the people had been urged to bring a week's supply of food with them. But in order to keep some of our camps from going without food over a day, Western members of our staff and committee have had to haul bags of rice to these places in their private cars after dark!

Besides the starvation facing the people if these services cannot be extended quickly, there is the stirring up of the people. Some families have had their houses entered, robbed, and their women raped as much as five times in one night. Is it any wonder that the next morning they move out and try to find a safer place? And yesterday afternoon while three officers of your Army Supply Department were asking us to help get the telephone service started, a small number of telephone workers wearing our insignia were turned out of their houses in the Zone and are now scattered to unknown places in the Zone. If this process of terrorism continues, it will be next to impossible to locate workers to get the essential services started. *It is hard to see how starvation may be prevented amongst many of the 200,000 Chinese civilians if order is not restored at once among the Japanese soldiers in the city.*

Assuring you that we will be glad to cooperate in any way we can in caring for the civilian population of this city, I am,

Most respectfully yours,
JOHN H. D. RABE, Chairman.

Enclosures:
Explanation in Chinese.
Regulations in Chinese.
PS. Cases of disorders in the Zone committed by Japanese soldiers since yesterday noon will be filed later.

The preceding letter is firmer, almost peremptory, compared to the extremely conciliatory tone of the others. The situation was desperate and it is surprising that the only sentence emphasized was the concluding one in which the prospect of starvation for the 200,000 Chinese in the Zone was urgently indicated.

As the result of a strong verbal protest to Mr. Fukui on the afternoon of December 17, guards had been promised at the eight refugee camps on American Mission property. They did not arrive but the fact they were expected made the first incident referred to in the following letter difficult for the Westerners involved to understand.

DOCUMENT No. 7 (Z 10, Z 11, and Z 12)
INTERNATIONAL COMMITTEE FOR NANKING SAFETY ZONE
5 Ninghai Road
December 18, 1937.

The Imperial Japanese
Embassy, Nanking.

For the kind attention of:
Mr. Kiyoshi Fukui,
Second Secretary to the Japanese Embassy.

DEAR SIRS:

We are very sorry to trouble you again but the sufferings and needs of the 200,000 civilians for whom we are trying to care make it urgent that we try to secure action from your military authorities to stop the present disorder among Japanese soldiers wandering through the Safety Zone.

There is no time or space here to go into the cases that are pouring in faster than we can type them out. But last night Dr. Bates of our Committee went to the University of Nanking dormitories to sleep in order to protect the one thousand women that fled there yesterday because of attacks in their homes. He found no gendarmerie on guard there nor at the new University library building. When at 8 p.m. Mr. Fitch and Dr. Smythe took Rev. W. P. Mills to Ginling College to sleep in a house near the gate (as one or more of us have been doing every night since the 14th in order to protect the three thousand women and children, yesterday augmented to four thousand by the panic), we were seized roughly by a searching squad and detained for over an hour. The officer had the two women in charge of Ginling College, Miss Minnie Vautrin and Mrs. Chen, with a friend, Mrs. Twinem, lined up at the gate and kept them there in the cold and the men pushed them around roughly. The officer insisted there were soldiers in the compound and he wanted to find them and shoot them. Finally, he let us go home but would not let Rev. Mills stay so we do not know what happened after we left.

This, combined with the marching off of the men at the Ministry of Justice on December 16 (see separate "Memorandum"), among which were several hundred civilian men to our positive knowledge and fifty of our uniformed police, has made us realize that, unless something is done to clear up this situation, the lives of all the civilian men in our Zone are at the mercy of the temperament of searching captains.

With the panic that has been created among the women who are now flocking by the thousands to our American instiution for protection, the men are being left more and more alone. (For instance, there were 600 people in the old Language School at Siao T'ao Yuen up till December 15. But because so many women were raped there on the night of December 15, four hundred women and children moved to Ginling College, leaving two hundred men.) These public institutional buildings were originally listed to accommodate 35,000 people; now, because of panic among the women, this has increased to 50,000 although two buildings have been emptied of men; the Ministry of Justice and the Supreme Court.

If this panic continues, not only will our housing problem become more serious but the food problem, and the question of finding workers will seriously increase. This morning one of your representatives, Mr. K. Kikuchi, was at our office asking for workers for the electric light plant. We had to reply that we could not even get our own workers out to do anything. We are only able to keep rice and coal supplied to these large concentrations of people by Western members of our Committee and Staff driving trucks for rice and coal. Our Food Commissioner has not dared leave his house for two days. The second man on our Housing Commission had to see two women in his family at 23 Hankow Road raped last night at supper time by Japanese soldiers. Our Associate Food Commissioner, Mr. Sone (a Theological Professor), has had to convey trucks with rice and leave the 2,500 people in families at his Nanking Theological Seminary to look out for themselves. Yesterday, in broad daylight, several women at the Seminary were raped right in the middle of a large room filled with men, women, and children! We twenty-two Westerners cannot feed 200,000 Chinese civilians and protect them night and day. That is the duty of the Japanese authorities. If you can give them protection, we can help feed them!

There is another matter that is in the minds of the Japanese officers searching the Zone: they think the place is full of "plainclothes soldiers." We have notified you several times of the presence of soldiers who disarmed and entered the Zone on the afternoon of December 13. But now we can safely assure you that there are no groups of disarmed Chinese soldiers in the Zone. Your searching squads have cleaned out all of them and many civilians along with them.

For the good of all concerned, we would beg to make the following constructive suggestions:

I. *Control of Soldiers.*

1. We repeat our request of yesterday for patrols of gendarmerie for the Zone night and day.

2. In our letter of December 16, we asked that guards be placed at entrances to the Zone to keep out wandering soldiers at night. This

has not been done. But we hope the Japanese Army will find some way to prevent soldiers from robbing, raping, and killing the civilian population especially at night, when soldiers might be confined to their barracks.

3. Until general order can be restored among the soldiers, will you please station sentries at the entrances to our nineteen larger concentrations of refugees. These sentries should be instructed to be responsible for preventing soldiers climbing over the walls of the compounds as well. (See list of "Refugee Camps" attached.)

4. We would also respectfully request that a proclamation in Japanese be put at each of these refugee camps describing what they are and ordering Japanese soldiers not to molest these poor people.

II. *Searching.*

1. Since our refugee camps seem to be misunderstood by captains of searching squads, we suggest that today we will be glad to have a high officer of the Japanese Army accompany one of our housing men to each of the eighteen Refugee Camps and see them in daylight.

2. Since we know there are no groups of disarmed soldiers in the Zone and there has been no sniping in the Zone at any time; and since, furthermore, search of both Refugee Camps and private houses has been carried out many times and each time means robbery and rape; we would venture to suggest that the Army's desires to prevent any former Chinese soldier's hiding in the Zone can now be accomplished by the patrols by the gendarmeries mentioned above.

3. We venture to make these suggestions because we sincerely believe that if the civilian population is left alone for two or three days, they will resume their normal daily life in the Zone, food and fuel can be transported, shops will open, and workers will appear looking for work. These workers can then help start the essential services of electricity, water, and telephones.

III. *Police that have been taken away.*

Yesterday we called your attention to the fact that fifty uniformed police had been taken from the Ministry of Justice, and that forty-five "volunteer police" had also been marched off. We now must add that forty of our uniformed police stationed at the Supreme Court were also taken. The only stated charge against them was made at the Ministry of Justice where the Japanese officer said they had taken in soldiers after the place had been searched once, and, therefore, they were to be shot. As pointed out in the accompanying "Memorandum on the Incident at the Ministry of Justice," Western members of our Committee take full responsibility for having put some civilian men and women in there because they had been driven out of other places by Japanese soldiers.

Yesterday, we requested that the 450 uniformed police assigned to the Zone be now organized into a new police force for the city under Japanese direction. At the same time, we trust the above-mentioned ninety uniformed police will be restored to their positions as policemen and that the forty-six volunteer police will either be returned to our office or we be informed their whereabouts as workers. We have on file a complete list of the 450 uniformed police assigned to the Zone so can help you in this process.

Trusting that you will pardon our venturing to make these suggestions, and assuring you of our willingness to cooperate in every way for the welfare of the civilians in the city, I am

Most respectfully yours,

JOHN H. D. RABE, Chairman.

Enclosure:
"Memorandum on Incident at Ministry of Justice"
"List of Refugee Camps in Safety Zone."

REFUGEE CAMPS IN THE NANKING SAFETY ZONE
as of December 17, 1937.

	Name of Building	Number of Refugees	Sex
1.	Old Ministry of Communications	10,000 or more	Families
2.	Wutaishan Primary School	1,640	Families
3.	Hankow Road Primary School	1,000	Families
4.	Military College	3,500	Families
5.	Nanking Language School at Siao Tao Yuen	200	Men
6.	Military Chemical Shops (back of Overseas Building)	4,000	Families
7.	University Middle School	6,000-8,000	Families
8.	Bible Teachers' Training School	3,000	Families
9.	Overseas Building	2,500	Families

Name of Building	Number of Refugees	Sex
10. Nanking Theological Seminary	2,500	Families
11. Ministry of Justice	empty	
12. Supreme Court	empty	
13. Sericulture Building at U. of N.	4,000	Families
14. Library Building at U. of N.	2,500	Families
15. German Club	500	Families
16. Ginling College	4,000	Women and children
17. Law College	500	Families
18. Rural Leaders' Training School	1,500	Families
19. Shansi Road Primary School	1,000	Families
20. University of Nanking dormitories	1,000	Women and children
Total persons	49,340—51,340	

MEMORANDUM ON THE INCIDENT AT THE MINISTRY OF JUSTICE

On the morning of December 16, a group of Japanese soldiers under an officer came to the Ministry of Justice and insisted on marching off most of the men to be shot—at least, that is what the officer said he was going to do with them. He also marched out all the police after seriously manhandling the Police Captain. There were probably fifty because that was the assignment to that station.

Two days previously, December 14th, a Japanese officer came into the Ministry of Justice and inspected half of the group, from which they took about 200—300 whom the officer claimed were soldiers and left 350 men whom they acknowledged to be civilians. This first search of half of the men in the building was very carefully carried out. The remaining half, which the officer did not inspect that day, were quartered in a separate part of the building and he promised to come back the next day, December 15, to inspect them and remove such soldiers as they might find among them. No officer came on the 15th to sort them. But on the 16th, an officer came and declared that they had taken all the soldiers at the time of the first

APPENDIX D 187

search on the 14th. Because he found some soldiers in this group on the 16th (including the half which had *not* been previously inspected), the officer declared that the police and we had put soldiers in there since the first inspection.

The only persons we added to this group was a number of civilians, that had been forced out of other houses by Japanese soldiers, who were taken to the Ministry of Justice by Mr. McCallum of the University Hospital, and Dr. M. S. Bates of our Committee. The fact that they found soldiers in the group on the 16th was *not* because the Committee had added any soldiers to the group, but because the Japanese soldiers had *failed* to inspect the second half of the group on the 15th as planned.

This whole incident on the morning of December 16th was observed by Mr. James McCallum of the University Hospital and by Mr. Charles Riggs of our Committee and Associate Housing Commissioner. During the process, the officer threatened Mr. Riggs with his sword three times and finally hit him hard over the heart twice with his fist. All Mr. Riggs was trying to do was to explain to the officer the situation described above in order to prevent civilians being mistaken for former soldiers.

(Signed) LEWIS S. C. SMYTHE,
Secretary, International Committee for Nanking Safety Zone.
Nanking, December 18, 1937.

On the afternoon of the 18th members of the Japanese Embassy and Japanese officers were shown cases of disorder in process. Conditions were so bad in the Safety Zone that the Chairman and Secretary of the Zone pleaded with Consul-General Okazaki to ask the Japanese Commander to order his troops out of the Zone before night. Nothing was done.

Hence early on Sunday morning after a dreadful night, the Director (Mr. Fitch), the Secretary, Dr. Bates and Dr. Wilson called on the Japanese Embassy and were received by Mr. Tanaka. Dr. Wilson presented a letter telling what had happened at the University Hospital during the night and they all pleaded with Mr. Tanaka to impress upon the Military the seriousness of the situation. The following letter was sent with a file of cases that afternoon:

DOCUMENT No. 8 (Z 13)

INTERNATIONAL COMMITTEE FOR NANKING SAFETY ZONE

5, Ninghai Road
December 19, 1937.
5 p.m.

The Imperial Japanese Embassy,
Nanking.

DEAR SIRS:

I am very sorry to have to present to you herewith a continuation of the "Cases of Disorders by Japanese Soldiers in the Safety Zone," being cases numbered sixteen to seventy. As indicated in the note, these are only a part of the cases that have come to our attention. Mr. Sperling (our Inspector-General), Mr. Kroeger, Mr. Hatz, and Mr. Riggs spend a good deal of their time escorting Japanese soldiers out of houses. These men do not have time to even dictate most of their cases.

I am also very regretful to have to report that the situation today is as bad as ever. One officer did come over in our area near Ninghai Road and cuff a large number of soldiers that were committing disorders. But that does not stop it!

Mr. Rabe asked me to apologize for his not coming this time, but he has three hundred women and children who have sought safety in his yard and felt he could not leave them.

We sincerely trust that the sentries will be placed at the eighteen Refugee Camps we listed to you yesterday and at the University Hospital, as requested by Dr. Wilson this morning. This will provide at least nineteen cases of safety in a sea of depredation and protect one-third or one-fourth of the population.

With kindest personal regards, I am,

Most respectfully yours,
(Signed) LEWIS S. C. SMYTHE,
Secretary.

APPENDIX D

Dr. Wilson's letter read as follows:

University Hospital,
Nanking.
December 19, 1937.

To the Officers of the Japanese Embassy,
Nanking.

SIRS:

I respectfully beg to call to your attention an incident occurring last night, December 18, at the University Hospital where we have over one hundred and fifty patients together with nurses, doctors and hospital staff and where in the past we have been privileged to serve various members of the staff of the Japanese Embassy with medical care.

Three soldiers entered the hospital compound by the rear door and tramped up and down the hospital corridors. This was at approximately 8 p.m., Miss Hynds, a sixty-three-year-old American nurse, met them and accompanied them. They took her watch in spite of her protestations that it was her own. They also took several (six) other watches and three fountain pens. Two of them then departed and the third disappeared without leaving.

At nine fifteen my attention was called to the fact that a Japanese soldier was in the nurse's dormitory. I went there with a lantern and found one soldier in a room with six nurses. He was partially dressed and I found that he had been in bed with three of the nurses before I arrived. All the nurses in the building were terrified beyond description.

Whereas heretofore we had considered that being a hospital we would be immune to this sort of incident and had not asked particularly for a guard at the hospital gates we would now like to place the matter in your hands with the request that such a guard be granted or other steps be taken to prevent the recurrence of any such proceeding.

Respectfully yours,
(Signed) ROBERT O. WILSON, M.D.

Numerous fires broke out in various parts of the city shortly after the Japanese took over and an investigation as to origin of these conflagrations was undertaken by the International Committee. This investigation showed that in many cases the fires must have been started deliberately by the Japanese troops, who used chemical strips for the purpose. On December 21 the following petition, signed by twenty-two foreign residents of Nanking, was submitted to the Japanese Embassy:

DOCUMENT No. 9 (Z 15)

Nanking, China.
December 21, 1937.

The Imperial Japanese Embassy,
Nanking.

DEAR SIRS:

We come to petition in the name of humanity that the following steps be taken for the welfare of the 200,000 civilians in Nanking:

1. That the burning of large sections of the city be stopped and what remains of the city be spared from either reckless or systematic burning.

2. That the disorderly conduct of Japanese troops in the city, which has caused so much suffering to the civilian population for one week, be immediately stopped.

3. In view of the fact that the looting and burning have brought the business life of the city to a standstill and consequently reduced the whole civilian population to one vast refugee camp, and in view of the fact that the International Committee has reserve food supplies to feed these 200,000 people one week only, we most earnestly beg you to take immediate steps to restore normal conditions of civilian life in order that the food and fuel supply of the city may be replenished.

The present situation is automatically and rapidly leading to a serious famine. We plead for the bare essentials of normal life: housing, security and food.

Most respectfully submitted,
THE FOREIGN COMMUNITY OF NANKING.
(Signed by 22 Foreigners.)

APPENDIX D 191

DOCUMENT No. 10 (Z 17)
FINDINGS REGARDING BURNING OF NANKING CITY
December 21, 1937

Conditions on the night of December 20.

Members of the Committee investigated the fire in the Zone on the night of December 19. One house at 16 Ping Tsang Hsiang had been set on fire by Japanese soldiers. Mr. Sperling with a fire officer of the Fire Brigade of the Safety Zone went to the fire but our pumps and fire equipment had been taken away several days before by the Japanese soldiers. During the day the buildings on the corner of Chung Shan Lu and Pao Tai Chieh had been burned out. And in the evening there were observed a number of fires in direction of Kuo Fu Lu.

On the afternoon of December 20 between 5 and 6 p.m. Mr. Fitch and Dr. Smythe went down Pao Tai Chieh and around south to Taiping Lu, on which they proceeded south of Peh Hsia Lu to where the streets were crowded from curb to curb with Japanese Army trucks and autos loading out goods. Down as far as Peh Hsia Lu, beginning from the creek just south of Kiukiang Road, they found groups of fifteen or twenty Japanese soldiers apparently under lower officers on both sides of the streets watching burning buildings, or clearing goods out of stores, and in other shops soldiers were seen building bonfires on the floors.

They then went over to Chung Hwa Lu and there found the same work in progress and the northern half of the Y.M.C.A. building in flames. Quite evidently this was set from the inside because there was no fire in any other buildings right around the Y.M.C.A. building. Japanese sentries paid no attention to them.

Later in the evening of the 20, about 9 p.m. Mr. Kroeger and Mr. Hatz drove down Chung Cheng Lu to Peh Hsia Lu, then east to Chung Hwa Lu but were prevented from proceeding southward by a Japanese sentry. The Y.M.C.A. building was about burned down. They then proceeded to Taiping Lu where they turned north and found about ten fires in progress on both sides of the road. Other buildings were already in ashes. They turned west on Chung Shan Tung Lu but observed a big fire about the corner of Tung Hai Lu and Kuo Fu Lu. When they came to the corner of Chung Shan Lu and Kiukiang Lu they observed a big fire on the north side of Kiukiang Lu. There a military patrol prevented their proceeding eastward. There were many soldiers about but none trying to stop the fire. Rather they were carrying away goods.

Signatures of observers of above conditions:

C. Kroeger	G. A. Fitch	M. S. Bates
Rupert Hatz	Eduard Sperling	Lewis S. C. Smythe

By the turn of the year the Committee apparently had lost hope of getting action on general lines and so they tackled individual cases by letter as in one of January 4:

DOCUMENT No. 11 (Z 27)

INTERNATIONAL COMMITTEE FOR NANKING SAFETY ZONE

5, Ninghai Road
January 4, 1938.
11 a.m.

The Japanese Embassy,
Nanking.

DEAR SIRS:

We are sorry to trouble you about another case, but since there are five other women involved there may be a chance of rescuing them. You will note in the short list of cases herewith presented (Cases 176-179) that case No. 178 is that of six women taken from one of our refugee centers. This woman has been brought to the University Hospital and you may see her there.

Would you be willing to go with some of us to see her and, if possible, learn more carefully about the location of the other five? Then your military police might investigate and save the others.

Thanking you for your kind cooperation in these matters, I am,

Respectfully yours,

Chairman.

On the 7th January, however, they returned to the attack with courtesy and calmness:

DOCUMENT No. 12 (Z 28)

Nanking,
January 7, 1938.

Mr. Tokuyasu Fukuda,
Japanese Embassy,
Nanking.

DEAR MR. FUKUDA:

With reference to our conversation of yesterday afternoon, I wish to assure you that the International Committee desires earnestly the earliest possible restoration of order and normal conditions of life in Nanking. To this end the Committee would, I am sure, be glad to see the local Self-Government Association assume as speedily as possible all the usual functions of a local civic administration: policing, fire protection, sanitation, etc. The International Committee has, I am quite certain, no desire whatsoever to carry on any of these administrative duties which are normally assumed by competent local administrations.

Our Committee is primarily, and indeed I might say solely, a relief organization, formed for the special purpose of caring for civilians suffering from war conditions. Everywhere the lot of such people is recognized as so pitiable as to command sympathy and compassion. Several Committees with similar purpose have been formed during the present crisis, and to one of them, the Shanghai Committee, General Matsui himself made a contribution of $10,000. thus showing the approval by the highest Japanese military authorities of the work of such Committees.

Since the funds and supplies given to our Committee were entrusted to it for the specific purpose above mentioned, it seems to me that a special obligation rests upon our Committee to discharge this trust to the best of its ability. I do not feel therefore that we should turn over our funds or supplies to any other organization. We would be glad to cooperate with other organizations in the relief work, as we are now doing with the Red Swastika and the Red Cross, but we should carry full responsibility for the use to be made of our own resources. I am sure that you yourself will see the reasonableness of this position.

Furthermore, I may point out that our funds and supplies are very limited when compared with the need that exists. Even at best all that our Committee can do should be but a mere supplementation of a much larger and more adequate program which I personally hope the local Self-Government Association will undertake. Our Committee can do its bit, as the Red Swastika and the Red Cross are now doing, but we trust that the Self-Government Association will do much more than our own Committee or than either of those other groups. We hope also that the Japanese military authorities will cooperate, even more liberally than they are now doing, with the Self-Government Association in the provision of food and fuel for the refugees. Even so the combined efforts of all agencies will scarcely overtake the need.

In closing, let me say one thing more. It is evident that the simplest and at the same time the most effective relief measure would be the restoration of order and discipline among the soldiers. Until this is done the people cannot go back to their homes, business cannot be carried on, communications cannot be restored, nor public services such as water, lights, and telephone be resumed. Everything waits on this one matter. But in proportion as discipline is restored, the relief problem will become easier, and the re-establishment of normal conditions be made more feasible. I earnestly hope that the military authorities will make this restoration of order their first concern.

Believe me, with kindest regards,

Sincerely yours,

(Signed) JOHN H. D. RABE,
Chairman.

RESTORATION OF NORMAL CONDITIONS IN NANKING

1. *Necessity of order in other parts of the city outside of the Safety Zone.*

    (1) Many people want to but cannot go home under the present state of insecurity outside of the Zone.

(2) No shops dare open in such a state of disorder. Without shops how are people to buy rice and other essentials?
(3) Economic life in the Zone is almost entirely on the basis of consumption of previous resources. (There is no production going on, not even farming.) The longer this condition continues the more destitute people will we have on our hands. People must be given security so they can return to normal economic life of some kind.

2. *How to obtain the necessary order in other parts of the city.*
   (1) It is proposed that the population be moved back into other areas of the city, section by section. (For instance: the first section opened to the population might well be the area south of Han Chung Lu to the south wall bounded on the east by Chung Cheng Lu and Chung Hwa Lu. This is an area from which a large number of the population in the Zone came from and is an area in which there has been relatively less burning.)
   (2) Before the population is moved into a section that is to be opened for people to return to their homes and business, the following steps should be taken:
   a. All wandering soldiers should be excluded from the new area.
   b. A strong system of military police throughout the area should be put in operation to see that the area is clear of soldiers. Military police offices should be specified where people may safely report any disturbance by soldiers.
   c. Arrangements should be made for important rice shops to open the morning the section is opened to the population.
   d. City water should be turned on in the area and places made available for people to get water.
   e. A number of civilian police should be moved into the section and organized.

3. *Restoration of economic life.*
   (1) All economic services by the local population to the Army

should be put on a definite commercial basis instead of on the present basis of commandeering.
   a. To help in this process, the *Tze Chih Wei Yuan Hwei* will be glad to start coolie hire and employment agencies.

(2) As rapidly as order is restored, lines of communication for economic life in and out of the city should be opened.
   a. Free communication in and out of the various gates of the city should be established.
   b. Carts, trucks, and boats hauling goods or people should be able to move in perfect safety without fear of robbery or confiscation of either goods or vehicles.
   c. Rickshas and carriages should be able to operate on the streets safely.
   d. By the first of February, order in the farming areas near the city should be such that farmers can begin their spring work in perfect safety. (At present farmers inside the city wall do not dare to return to their homes and farm their garden patches.)

(3) In addition to these very minimum essentials listed above, banks, telephone, post office, telegraph, city railway and bus lines should be established. Railway and boat service should be started as soon as possible.

4. *Burning must stop.*

(1) It is now beyond the stage of shops—in which however many people also lived—and has been destroying houses in which people must live when they return to those areas of the city.

(2) Burning makes it more and more difficult for economic life to start or carry on. It is destroying the material resources of the community.

(3) It destroys electric wires and water pipes.

(4) Psychologically makes people feel more insecure: fear of being burned out tomorrow or the day after they move back to their old homes.

Now follow two letters on foodstuffs that show how serious the position was becoming:

Document No. 13 (Z 37)

INTERNATIONAL COMMITTEE FOR NANKING SAFETY ZONE

5 Ninghai Road,
January 13, 1938.

Mr. Fukui,
Acting Consul-General,
Nanking.
Dear Sir:

We have concluded arrangements long under way for purchase from the Shanghai Commercial and Savings Bank of a supply of wheat and rice, as below, and would greatly appreciate your assistance in securing the necessary permits for us to take delivery, as we are in urgent need of further food-stuffs for our relief work. This grain will be used for free distribution and not for sale. We understand that the godowns in which these stocks are stored have been sealed by either the Military or Navy, but as they are private stocks, bearing the seal of the Bank, we trust there will be no difficulty in securing their release.

In Godown No. 1 San Chiao Ho: 5,000 bags of wheat
" " " " " 2,000 " " rice
" " " 2 Hah Si Men: 4,000 " " wheat
" " " 4 Hsiakwan: 1,000 " " rice

Thanking you for your kind attention to this matter, I am,

Faithfully yours,

(Signed) G. A. Fitch,
Director.

DOCUMENT No. 14 (Z 35)

5 Ninghai Road,
Nanking.
January 14, 1938.

Mr. Tokuyasu Fukuda,
Japanese Embassy,
Nanking.

MY DEAR MR. FUKUDA:

On December 21 members of the foreign community called the attention of the Japanese authorities to the fact that food and fuel supplies available for the civilian population in Nanking were very inadequate and asked them to take suitable steps to cope with the situation. On December 27 I talked this matter over with Mr. Fukui, especially regarding rice and coal. Mr. Fukui replied that the Army preferred to handle the rice through the *Tze Chih Wei Yuan Hwei* but that he would help us to secure coal for soup kitchens. However, a coal yard was assigned to the *Tze Chih Wei Yuan Hwei* to use for relief purposes. This yard contained 550 tons of coal when we first investigated it on December 27. But because much of the coal had been hauled away by others in the meantime, only 100 tons was secured for soup kitchens.

At the same time that we were negotiating with Mr. Fukui, Major T. Ishida of the Army Supply Department voluntarily told Mr. Sperling that he would sell us plenty of rice and flour for relief purposes. Mr. Kroeger and Mr. Sperling approached Major Ishida on the matter and he offered us 5,000 bags of rice and 10,000 bags of flour. We gave him an order for 3,000 bags of rice and 5,000 bags of flour on January 7. He also promised to sell us 600 tons of coal for soup kitchens. Three days later when Mr. Kroeger went back to arrange delivery of the rice, Major Ishida said he could not sell us rice, flour or coal because it was to be distributed through the *Tze Chih Wei Yuan Hwei*.

On January 8, the *Tze Chih Wei Yuan Hwei* told us that they had been assigned 1,250 bags of rice for free distribution outside of the Zone and 10,000 bags of rice to sell, and asked us to help them truck it. We organized this on Sunday, the 9th, and had five trucks

APPENDIX D 199

on the job Monday morning. In the meantime they had secured permission to sell the 1,250 bags assigned to distribution and use a similar amount from assignment of 10,000 bags for free distribution later. The hauling of the 1,250 bags was completed in two days and sold as rapidly as it arrived. When the men supervising the trucking started to get the other 10,000 bags on the 12th, they were told that that assignment had been turned down and that now only 1,000 bags could be secured every three days. Already two days' delay had been used in negotiations about the matter. A check-up yesterday, January 13, shows that all the coal in coal yards which we had pointed out to you on December 27 as places where coal might be made available for civilian use, has either been hauled away or burned. (These seven yards on December 27 contained over 2,000 tons of coal.)

We are glad to cooperate with you and the *Tze Chih Wei Yuan Hwei* in caring for this civilian population which now has no economic basis of support. This was evidenced by closing our rice shop when the *Tze Chih Wei Yuan Hwei* asked us to on January 10 and on the same day in helping them truck the rice assigned to them—from which our soup kitchens and camps did *not* receive a single bag.

We understand that you registered 160,000 people without including children under ten years of age, and in some sections without including older women. Therefore there are probably 250,000 to 300,000 civilians in the city. To feed this population on normal rations of rice would require 2,000 *tan* of rice per day (or, 1,600 bags per day). From this it will be clear that the proposed 1,000 bags for every three days is less than one-third the amount of rice needed. Up to the present the people have gotten along very largely on their private stores of rice but that is being rapidly used up and the demand for purchasing rice has risen very rapidly since January 1st. There should immediately be made available for purchase by the people at least 1,000 bags of rice per day and that should be increased to 1,600 bags per day as soon as possible.

In addition to this there should be flour available for purchase in large quantities and 2,000 tons of coal, for one or two months' supply, as well as other fuel. Deliberate and efficient planning is necessary in order to prevent great suffering in this winter weather.

I write therefore to enquire what the state of affairs actually is, and why the arrangements previously made have been cancelled. The people must eat and when they are deprived of rice, or of the fuel with which to cook it, they are reduced to a bitter condition indeed. Permit me to ask you to straighten out this matter at once with the military authorities so that there will be a dependable supply of rice and fuel made constantly available for the people. Whether the rice and fuel comes through our own Committee or through the *Tze Chih Wei Yuan Hwei* makes no difference to us. What our Committee does desire is that some adequate supply of these essentials of life be made available to the people. It would be well to have this done so far as possible on a commercial basis.

In closing, let me add a word. If you have any suggestions as to how the service which our Committee is rendering can be improved, we shall be most happy to have them.

With kindest regards and thanks for your untiring help in these matters, I am,

Respectfully yours,
(Signed) JOHN H. D. RABE,
Chairman International Committee
for Nanking Safety Zone.

The urgency was further emphasized by a telegram to the National Christian Council and letter to the three foreign representatives by then in Nanking: Messrs. Allison (American), Prideaux-Brune (British), and Rosen (German).

DOCUMENT No. 15

Boynton National Christian Council Shanghai.

Food question more serious because no regular supply available civilian population. Only twenty-two hundred bags rice one thousand bags flour released for sale from large stocks on hand to two hundred fifty thousand people since December thirteenth. Population has existed on private family stocks which are now running out. We are feeding fifty thousand daily free rice. Request to truck in rice wheat purchased here and request for necessary passes to ship six hundred

tons foodstuffs from Shanghai turned down. Please try negotiations Shanghai. If you can buy Chinese green beans Shanghai get permission and ship one hundred tons as soon as possible. Go ahead raising funds. We will find way to use them. Release. Fitch.
January 18, 1938.
3 p.m.

DOCUMENT NO. 16 (B Z 40)

January 19, 1938.

Mr. Allison, American Embassy,
Mr. Prideaux-Brune, British Embassy,
Dr. Rosen, German Embassy,
Nanking.

GENTLEMEN:

You have each individually expressed a friendly interest in the problem of seeing that the 250,000 civilians in this city are fed. As indicated in Mr. Smythe's letter to Mr. Allison on January 17, of which you all have copies, we have pressed three propositions on the Japanese: (1) speed up the commercial distribution of rice, flour and coal through the *Tze Chih Wei Yuan Hwei;* (2) give the International Committee passes for trucking in 3,000 bags of rice and 9,000 bags of wheat (in Hsiakwen, San Chia Ho, and outside Hansimen) we had purchased for relief purposes from the Shanghai Commercial and Savings Bank; and (3) give the International Committee the necessary passes for shipping 600 tons of supplementary foodstuffs from Shanghai.

Yesterday Mr. Smythe went for the third time to ask an answer to these propositions. Mr. Fukui referred him to Mr. Tanaka. So Mr. Smythe and Mr. Fitch interviewed Mr. Tanaka. He said the Army had confiscated the rice and wheat in the said godowns. When they pointed out that it was private stocks instead of military he said that the Army had probably used it for the civilian population. Then they asked if the Japanese authorities would give us permission to ship 3,000 bags of rice from Shanghai. He said, "No." With regard to that and the shipment of 600 tons of supplementary foodstuffs from Shanghai he said there were no boats. They told him it could be brought on Japanese boats. He said their boats were busy for the military. They suggested the Japanese let a British boat bring it. He did not reply. So they asked him what the Japanese proposed to do about it.

To this question, Mr. Tanaka replied that the Army would assume responsibility for feeding the civilian population. So then we told him that so far the Army had only assigned 2,200 bags of rice and 1,000 bags of flour for sale to the civilian population since December 13. He thought they had done more but had no figures. (The Army let the *Tze Chih Wei Yuan Hwei* have 1,200 bags of rice on January 10th. On the 17th the Army gave them another assignment of 1,000 bags of rice and 1,000 bags of flour to be sold in the southern part of the city. Both of these assignments the International Committee has had to help them truck because the Army made no offer to truck it.) In concluding the interview, Mr. Smythe asked Mr. Tanaka if he should inform me that they refused both our requests for permission to haul rice and wheat purchased in Hsiakwan etc. and our request for permission to ship foodstuffs from Shanghai. He said, "Yes."

With regard to the Shanghai consignment, we immediately telegraphed to Mr. Boynton of the National Christian Council in Shanghai (who has been corresponding with us about the matter) as per enclosed telegram signed by Mr. Fitch. This was to see what could be done in Shanghai.

I do not know how much you gentlemen want to do in this matter, but we are attempting to keep you informed of developments and pass on to you the best suggestions that we can make. We do not think it advisable at this juncture to ask you to press for the Japanese to grant our two requests. But since Mr. Tanaka said the Japanese Army wanted to feed the civilian population itself, you could informally suggest to the Japanese, "Now let's see you do it!"

That, or better the restoration of order and communications so commercial distribution of rice can function normally, is the only solution of the problem. The International Committee is only interested in arousing the Army's awareness of the seriousness of the problem and in the meantime provide relief in the form of free food to those who are unable to buy.

What seems to be necessary is to impress upon the Army what it means to assume responsiblity for feeding this population. So far they have only been playing at it with an occasional grant of 1,000 bags of rice which they sell to the *Tze Chih Wei Yuan Hwei*. Here is what feeding this population really means:

(1) A regular supply of rice to the extent of 2,000 *tan* (or 1,600 bags) of rice *per day,* or approximately the same weight of flour. (250,000 people at the normal daily consumption of one *tan* per 100 adults per day would be 2,500 *tan* per day, but small children in the population would not need so much per day.)

(2) At least 40-50 tons of coal per day and other fuels.

(3) Since the *Tze Chih Wei Yuan Hwei* does not have the trucks available for trucking in this much supplies every day and the Army has trucks standing around all over town, the Army should deliver this rice, flour and fuel to the *Tze Chih Wei Yuan Hwei* shops. (In our negotiations with Major Ishida of the Army Supply Department to buy such supplies, he was quite willing to deliver to us. That arrangement broke down because of instructions from outside his department.)

In addition to the rice and flour there should be some provision for supplementary foodstuffs in order to reduce the danger of disease and possible epidemics. This was our object in getting such supplies from Shanghai. The Army could do this.

If the *Tze Chih Wei Yuan Hwei* is assured of adequate supplies, they can manage the distribution.

Of course, as any efficient government would do, the Japanese must provide adequate protection to civilians returning to their homes as well as provide for regular commercial distribution of food and fuel.

Thanking you for your friendly interest in this matter, I am,

Most respectfully yours,
(Signed) JOHN H. D. RABE.
Chairman, International Committee
for Nanking Safety Zone.

On January 26 and 28 the Committee sent the foreign representatives urgent requests for assistance. The first one follows:

DOCUMENT No. 17 (Z 43)

INTERNATIONAL COMMITTEE FOR NANKING SAFETY ZONE

5 Ninghai Road
January 26, 1938.

Mr. Allison, American Embassy,
Mr. Prideaux-Brune, British Embassy,
Dr. Rosen, German Embassy,
Nanking.

GENTLEMEN:

We called the attention of the Japanese authorities to food supplies assigned to the International Committee in our letter of December 14 and interviews on December 15. At their request we pointed out the locations of the rice. But since then all our representations to the Japanese authorities on this question have been ignored.

Therefore we are presenting you herewith the facts regarding the food supplies assigned to the International Committee for use in feeding the population in the Safety Zone.

In his letter of November 30, former Mayor Ma promised the Committee 30,000 *tan* of rice, and in another letter of December 3 he gave us 10,000 bags of flour. Later he verbally promised us another 10,000 bags of flour.

On December 2 we received an assignment voucher for 15,000 bags of rice and on December 5 another assignment voucher for 5,009 bags of rice. Of this amount we were able to haul in only 8,476 bags and assigned 600 bags to refugees in Hsiakwan, or a total receipt of 9,076 bags containing 11,345 *tan*. But since the bag vouchers only totalled 20,009 bags, we can only claim 10,933 bags of rice as still coming to us when the Japanese took the city on December 13.

We did not get any of the 10,000 bags of flour for which we had assignment vouchers. We hauled in 1,000 bags of flour but that was a separate gift from the Ta Tung Flour Mills arranged by the Asiatic Petroleum Company.

APPENDIX D

This matter is summarized in the following table:

	Assignment Vouchers	Actually received	Confiscated by Japanese authorities
Rice	20,009 bags	9,076 bags	10,933 bags x 96 kilograms
Flour	10,000 bags	none	10,000 bags x 50 lbs.

You will note that this amount, 10,933 bags of rice and 10,000 bags of flour, was confiscated by the Japanese authorities from an international relief committee.

We would be pleased if you would support our claim in this matter.

Thanking you for your continued help, I am,

Respectfully yours,
(Signed) JOHN H. D. RABE,
Chairman.

When Mr. S. Hidaka, Counsellor of the Japanese Embassy, was in Nanking the Committee asked Mr. Allison to approach him informally on a number of outstanding questions, including their claim to stores of rice and flour confiscated by the Japanese Army. In reply Mr. Hidaka asked whether the Committee would be willing to cooperate with the local Self-Government Committee in the distribution of such supplies. The following letter was the Committee's answer:

DOCUMENT No. 18 (Z 54)

INTERNATIONAL COMMITTEE FOR NANKING SAFETY ZONE

5 Ninghai Road
February 6, 1938.

Mr. John M. Allison,
American Embassy,
Nanking.

MY DEAR MR. ALLISON:

The International Committee is concerned only with carrying out its responsibilities for using on behalf of civilians in Nanking the money and supplies given to it. Therefore the Committee is ready to distribute its rice in cooperation with the Self-Government Committee, or under the name of the latter.

However, the International Committee cannot rightly shirk the duty of arranging the actual methods of distribution, which greatly affects the degree of service rendered to the needy population. The Committee must also point out that the attitudes of large sections of foreign opinion both in China and abroad would be unfavorably affected by confiscation of means legally given to the Committee.

It would seem that the position taken in the first paragraph is a fair and friendly solution of the problem.

Respectfully yours,
(Signed) JOHN H. D. RABE,
Chairman.

These representations were followed up by another letter to the Japanese Embassy under date of January 27:

DOCUMENT No. 19 (Z 44)

INTERNATIONAL COMMITTEE FOR NANKING
SAFETY ZONE

5 Ninghai Road
January 27, 1938

The Japanese Embassy,
Nanking.

Attention: Mr. Fukui

DEAR SIRS:

From the time of our first contact with the Japanese authorities in Nanking on December 14 up to the present, we have had frequent conversations with you about the local food situation. We made an early request to get delivery of the food supplies assigned to us by the former Nanking Municipality. Later we offered also to purchase supplies for relief work. However, this latter offer was refused by the authorities. In the meantime only very small additional supplies of rice have been available in the city. Therefore, since private rice stocks are now running low, and our own supplies are also being exhausted, we feel that we must urge upon you again our original request that we be allowed to secure all the food supplies assigned to us by the former Nanking Municipality.

Consequently, we are now writing to you stating the full facts in the case in order to clear up the matter.

In his letter of November 30, former Mayor Ma promised the International Committee 30,000 *tan* of rice, and in another letter of December 3 he gave us 10,000 bags of flour. Later he verbally promised us another 10,000 bags of flour at the press conference.

On December 2 we received an assignment voucher for 15,000 bags of rice and on December 5 another assignment voucher for 5,009 bags of rice. Of this amount we were able to haul in only 8,476 bags and assigned 600 bags to refugees in Hsiakwan, or a total receipt of 9,076 bags containing 11,345 *tan*. But since the bag vouchers only totalled 20,000 bags, we can only claim 10,933 bags of rice as still coming to us when the Japanese troops took the city on December 13.

We did not get any of the 10,000 bags of flour for which we had a written assignment. We hauled in 1,000 bags of flour but that was a separate gift from the Ta Tung Flour Mill arranged by the Asiatic Petroleum Company.

This matter is summarized in the following table:

	Assignment vouchers	*Actually received*	*Not secured either before or after December 13th.*
Rice	20,000 bags	9,076 bags	10,933 bags x 96 kilograms
Flour	10,000 bags	none	10,000 bags x 50 lbs.

You will note that the above food supplies were definitely assigned to an international relief committee for use in its relief work in Nanking.

We would be pleased if you would favor us with a written reply of how your authorities wish to handle this matter in order that it may be perfectly clear.

Thanking you for your continued help, I am,

Respectfully yours,
(Signed) JOHN H. D. RABE,
Chairman.

On January 28 the Japanese authorities threw the inhabitants of the Safety Zone into a state of consternation by announcing that plans had been made for their transfer to other parts of the city. The Committee's view of the situation was stated in the following communication from the Chairman to Dr. Rosen:

DOCUMENT No. 20 (Z 48)
INTERNATIONAL COMMITTEE FOR NANKING
SAFETY ZONE
5 Ninghai Road

Herr Dr. Rosen: January 30, 1938.
German Embassy,
Nanking.

MY DEAR DR. ROSEN,

In answer to your inquiries regarding the position of the International Committee at the present juncture, we briefly report as follows:

It is now common knowledge that on the afternoon of January 28 a responsible officer of the Special Service Organ, with the cooperation of the Self-Government Committee, informed leaders of refugee camps of plans for the prompt return of refugees to other parts of the city.

We heartily approve the announcement of specific measures for the better protection of residents throughout the city, and the provision of houses for those whose dwellings have been burned or who for other reasons need shelter in Nanking.

The International Committee has from the beginning of its relief work desired a return to normal living conditions as early as possible. The prolonged strain resulting from general insecurity and consequent crowding in the Safety Zone, has been highly unsatisfactory to us as a Committee and also as individuals. We have encouraged many Chinese to return to their homes in others parts of the city, and long ago gave instructions to the same effect in various refugee camps. Indeed, on several occasions the number of refugees in certain camps has fallen by reason of such efforts to return. But considerable numbers have come back into the refugee camps. Why is this?

The minimum needs for normal residence throughout the city are these: (1) Security against violence, raping, and robbery by soldiers.

(2) A regular and assured food supply, both of rice and flour in dependable centers of distribution, and of vegetables which cannot be provided until the surrounding country and the roads are safe. (3) Protection against fire, which from military hands has long continued to destroy homes and shops. If these simple needs can be met in actual experience, the people will rapidly go to their homes, which they desire to protect and use. But some time is needed to carry out the new measures of order and protection and to enable the people to realize that they can be safe.

Meanwhile the order that refugees must return by February 4 or they will be driven out from the refugee camps by soldiers, and that all merchants will be forcibly driven from the Refugee Zone, is a serious matter. We respectfully suggest for your consideration that this threat or use of violence arouses difficulties: (1) Resentful feelings among the people if they are pushed by bayonets from relative safety into danger. Such action seems contrary to the declared policy of the Japanese military and civil authorities to give kindly treatment and good conditions of life to the common people. (2) An unfavorable movement of world opinion, which is already watchful of conditions in Nanking and would severely judge any use of military force upon unarmed civilians. (3) Possibly an unfavorable attitude among foreign governments, some of whom are already concerned with the humanitarian aspects of the situation in Nanking, and would be still further disturbed by fresh difficulties. (4) Because of the points just mentioned, it would seem that the Japanese authorities in Tokyo would wish to avoid difficulties that would arise from the action proposed.

In cooperation with the purpose of restoring the city of Nanking to orderly conditions of life, we suggest that statements be made immediately to the public, in order to remove fear and increase confidence: (1) That the Japanese authorities and the Self-Government Committee are taking certain clearly specified steps to promote order and improve conditions in all parts of Nanking. (2) That progress in removal from the Safety Zone to other parts of the city should be prompt, but force will not be used. If "(1)" is carried out satisfactorily in practice, the people will return of their own accord and therefore force will be unnecessary.

The International Committee is glad to distribute its moderate resources according to needs and opportunities in any section of the city. It hopes earnestly improvement of conditions will within a few weeks lessen need for relief work in which it is interested. General security will automatically remove all need for a Safety Zone in any one section of the city. The International Committee is therefore considering a change of its name to something like the following: "Nanking Relief Committee." Such a name will more accurately indicate the functions of the Committee, particularly after the people can enjoy throughout the city the relatively good protection which the Japanese authorities have recently provided for the Safety Zone.

We trust we have made clear our main purpose of relief only, and of cooperation with practical measures of return of refugees to their homes. Likewise, our friendly anxiety over threats of force to compel return before general security is established.

Thanking you for your good help in this matter, I am

Respectfully yours,
(Signed) JOHN H. D. RABE,
Chairman.

Happily, as a result of representations made to Mr. Shinrokuro Hidaka, Counsellor of the Japanese Embassy, who had arrived in Nanking on a visit from Shanghai, the threatened eviction did not take place. In the following letter Mr. Rabe voices his appreciation of Mr. Hidaka's attitude:

DOCUMENT No. 21 (Z 35)
INTERNATIONAL COMMITTEE FOR NANKING
SAFETY ZONE

5 Ninghai Road

February 3, 1938.

Mr. Hidaka,
Japanese Embassy,
Nanking.

MY DEAR SIR:

I recall with friendly appreciation your assurance of yesterday that refugees will not be forcibly evicted from the present camps, and am

APPENDIX D 211

sure that this wise policy will obviate any danger of serious difficulties over the problem. You will of course realize the importance of securing the detailed cooperation of the military authorities to this end so that all possibility of misunderstanding may be averted. This is the more necessary because repeated and specific instructions were issued for removal by Friday, February 4, under threat of military compulsion and sealing of gates.

We are grateful for the new opportunities of friendly contact with the Japanese authorities, as provided by General Homma, yourself, and the expected arrival of Lieutenant-Colonel Hirota.

With kindest personal regards, I beg to remain,

Most respectfully yours,
(Signed) JOHN H. D. RABE,
Chairman.

This selection need not be made any longer except by the addition of a series of letters addressed between the 10th of January and 19th of February by the Committee to Mr. Allison which are self-explanatory and which are an indication of the sort of problem with which the Committee and the Foreign Representatives had to deal day after day during this whole period—roughly four months—during which conditions improved only with incredible slowness. As lately as early April cases of violence were still occurring.

DOCUMENT No. 22 (Z 32)

3 P'ing Ts'ang Hsiang,
Nanking.
January 10, 1938.

DEAR MR. ALLISON:

In reply to your request for confidential information regarding the status of the International Committee and the stand it has taken regarding any attempt to take over its resources, I will give you a brief summary of the developments.

Our letter of December 17 (File 29) was intended to make this clear to the Japanese authorities because Consul-General Katsuo Okazaki had called on the 16th to tell us that while they could not recognize us legally, they would deal with us as though they had recognized us. We stated on page 6 of the above letter:

"May we again reassure you that we have no interest in continuing any semi-administrative function left to us by the former Nanking City Government. We earnestly hope that you will kindly take up these functions as quickly as possible. Then we will become simply a relief organization."

However, regarding supplies, on December 15 the head of the Special Service Corps told us in an interview that we could keep the supplies we had (File 26).

On December 31 and January 1 we were confidentially informed that the Japanese Consul had informed the group organizing the *Tze Chih Wei Yuan Hwei* that they could have the supplies and money that the International Committee had. Consequently we thought out a statement of our position on January 3, as follows:

"We are a private organization for assistance to civilians who suffered from war conditions. This is what the food and money were given to us for. Because the money was given to this Committee, therefore, we continue this Committee but adapt use of resources to conditions around us. Such political services as we had were paid separately from our regular funds. (The police pay was not even turned over to us but handled separately by their office. We have supplied them with rice on the same basis as other refugees or volunteer workers. The three clerks that came to our organization from the City Government had a separate assignment of pay.)"

Consequently, when on the night of January 6, Mr. Tokuyasu Fukuda came to Mr. Rabe to tell him confidentially and informally that the Japanese Army authorities wanted all business in the future to be done through the *Tze Chih Wei Yuan Hwei* and would, therefore, like to take over all our funds and supplies, Mr. Rabe was ready to reply, and told him informally our position. But since Mr. Fukuda said he would be very pleased to have a personal letter from Mr. Rabe stating our position, Mr. Rabe called a meeting of the Standing Committee of the International Committee immediately and we decided to reply as is given in the letter by Mr. Rabe on January 7 to Mr. Fukuda (File 22, 29).

For the present there the matter rests. But on Saturday, January 8 the Japanese Army authorities wanted to come over and close our rice shop forcibly. So in discussion with the new Food Commissioner (under the *Tze Chih Wei Yuan Hwei*), Mr. Wang Ch'en-tien, yesterday, we volunteered to close our rice shop this morning. We had been anxious to do that for ten days but up until yesterday the *Tze Chih Wei Yuan Hwei* was not ready to take over sale of rice. However, we will continue our free distribution as before. We have arranged to start five trucks to haul the 10,000 bags of rice the Japanese Army has assigned them. That for commercial distribution we will charge hauling costs; that for free distribution (an extra 1,250 bags to be distributed *outside* the zone) we will haul free of charge.

One other step in the process of "freezing us out" is that this morning the head of the supply department of the Army, Major T. Ishida refused to carry out his former agreement to sell us 3,000 bags of rice and 5,000 bags of flour for relief purposes. We will not try to buy this from the *Tze Chih Wei Yuan Hwei*. But as long as they keep rice, flour and coal moving into either the Zone or other places available to the civilian population, we will be happy. We are anxious to reserve our supplies against a possible breakdown in these arrangements or any monopoly attempt to raise the price.

Thanking you for your interest in these matters affecting the welfare of the people of Nanking, I am

Most respectfully yours,
(Signed) LEWIS S. C. SMYTHE.

PS. I am enclosing herewith copies of:
1. Mr. Rabe's letter to Mr. Fukuda, January 7 (File Z 29).
2. "Restoration of Normal Conditions in Nanking" (File Z 30).

The second was a memorandum we were working out for the *Tze Chih Wei Yuan Hwei* and Mr. Fukuda asked Mr. Rabe for a copy of it.

DOCUMENT No. 23 (B Z 33)

5 Ninghai Road,
Nanking.
January 10, 1938.

DEAR MR. ALLISON,

Because Dr. Bates was the one who investigated the case in which Mr. Riggs was involved last night, I asked him to turn in a separate report to you. I have merely summarized it in this list of cases, "Notes about the Present Situation," Case No. 187. These "Notes" are a continuation of my "Cases of Disorders by Japanese Soldiers in the Safety Zone."

The first four cases show the danger to the civilian population where they live near military offices along Chung Shan Lu (Cases 180-183). Cases 184 and 186 show the difficulties that confront people that try to return to their homes. Case 185 shows lack of common decency or humanity in execution and what concerns us even more is the threat to the health of the population by the continued presence of dead bodies in the area, especially in ponds. So far we have been very fortunate to have no serious outbreak of sickness in the city. But if the present unsanitary measures go on, especially if the city water supply is not dependable, we all live in continual danger of a serious epidemic.

Case 187, as Dr. Bates has already pointed out, shows the character of some of the Military Police upon whom both we and the Chinese are dependent for the maintenance of order amongst the soldiers. Dr. Rosen told me today he had suggested that the Japanese should bring in a high grade group of military police, from Tokyo if necessary.

Hoping that some of this information may be of service to you, I am

Most respectfully yours,
(Signed) LEWIS S. C. SMYTHE.

APPENDIX D

In order to help eliminate the Japanese Army's misunderstanding of the Committee's continuing as a relief committee after disbanding the Zone as a Zone, the Committee changed its name as reported in the following letter[1]:

DOCUMENT No. 24 (Z 58)

NANKING INTERNATIONAL RELIEF COMMITTEE
5 Ninghai Road

February 19, 1938.

Mr. John M. Allison,
American Embassy,
Nanking.

MY DEAR MR. ALLISON,

On February 18 the International Committee for the Nanking Safety Zone decided that from henceforth it would operate under the name of "Nanking International Relief Committee" which is more in conformity with our present functions.

The Committee wishes to take this opportunity to thank your Embassy for its moral support of the Safety Zone from the days of first negotiations regarding the formation of the Zone to the present. We also deeply appreciate your humanitarian interest in the continuing relief work of the Committee.

Most respectfully yours,
(Signed) JOHN H. D. RABE,
Chairman.

Same letter to:
Mr. Jeffery, British Embassy.
Dr. G. Rosen, German Embassy.

[1] A similar letter to the Nanking Self-Government Committee.

APPENDIX E

THE NANKING "MURDER RACE"

ON DECEMBER 7, 1937, *the* Japan Advertiser, *an American-owned and edited English-language daily paper in Tokyo, published the following item:*

SUB-LIEUTENANTS IN RACE
TO FELL 100 CHINESE
RUNNING CLOSE CONTEST

Sub-lieutenant Toshiaki Mukai and Sub-lieutenant Takeshi Noda, both of the Katagiri unit at Kuyung, in a friendly contest to see which of them will first fell 100 Chinese in individual sword combat before the Japanese forces completely occupy Nanking, are well in the final phase of their race, running almost neck to neck. On Sunday when their unit was fighting outside Kuyung, the "score," according to the *Asahi*, was: Sub-lieutenant Mukai, 89, and Sub-lieutenant Noda, 78.

On December 14, 1937, the same paper published the following additional report:

CONTEST TO KILL FIRST 100 CHINESE
WITH SWORD EXTENDED WHEN BOTH
FIGHTERS EXCEED MARK

The winner of the competition between Sub-Lieutenant Toshiaki Mukai and Sub-Lieutenant Iwao Noda to see who would be the first to kill 100 Chinese with his Yamato sword has not been decided, the *Nichi Nichi* reports from the slopes of Purple Mountain, outside Nanking. Mukai has a score of 106 and his rival has dispatched 105 men, but the two contestants have found it impossible to determine which passed the 100 mark first. Instead of settling it with a discussion, they are going to extend the goal by 50.

Mukai's blade was slightly damaged in the competition. He explained that this was the result of cutting a Chinese in half, helmet and all. The contest was "fun," he declared, and he thought it a good thing that both men had gone over the 100 mark without knowing that the other had done so.

Early Saturday morning, when the *Nichi Nichi* man interviewed the sub-lieutenant at a point overlooking Dr. Sun Yat-sen's tomb, another Japanese unit set fire to the slopes of Purple Mountain in an attempt to drive out the Chinese troops. The action also smoked out Sub-Lieutenant Mukai and his unit, and the men stood idly by while bullets passed overhead.

"Not a shot hits me while I am holding this sword on my shoulder," he explained confidently.

APPENDIX F

HOW THE JAPANESE REPORTED CONDITIONS IN NANKING

L ITTLE OR NO *mention was made in Japanese papers of conditions in Nanking following the occupation by Japanese forces. A survey of English-language papers in Japan revealed no references to the accounts widespread in Shanghai and the world over reporting Japanese atrocities in Nanking or elsewhere. Some attempts, however, were made to picture Nanking as calm and quiet. The following, which appeared on January 8, 1938, in the Chinese-language paper* Sin Shun Pao (*New Shun Pao*), *published by the Japanese in Shanghai, is typical of such efforts.*

(Translation from Chinese)

JAPANESE TROOPS GENTLY SOOTHE REFUGEES

HARMONIOUS ATMOSPHERE OF NANKING DEVELOPS

The municipality of Nanking is still as the streets of the dead. The sun's merciful rays spread forth with partiality for the refugees' district in the northwest. The herds of refugees who fled for their lives from the midst of death, have met with the gentle soothing of the Japanese Army. They respectfully kneel by the side of the road in joyful thanks. Before the Japanese troops entered the city, they suffered from the oppression of the anti-Japanese armies of the

APPENDIX F

Chinese. Indeed, not a grain of rice or millet could reach their hands; the sick could not get medical aid; the hungry could not get food. The sufferings of plain good citizens were infinitely miserable.

Fortunately the Imperial Army entered the city, put their bayonets into their sheaths, and stretched forth merciful hands in order to examine and to heal, diffusing grace and favor to the excellent true citizens. In the region west of the Japanese Embassy, many thousands of herded refugees cast off their former absurd attitude of opposing Japan, and clasped their hands in congratulation for receiving assurance of life. Men and women, old and young, bent down to kneel in salutation to the Imperial Army expressing their respectful intention. This for Chinese has an especial ceremonial significance, and it certainly could not have appeared except from a sincere heart and with a genuine purpose. Within the Refugee Zone they (Japanese soldiers) gave out military bread, cakes, and cigarettes to refugees of both sexes and all ages, all of whom were greatly pleased and who gave thanks. Around the well and Japanese barracks gifts of good will, politely given to the poor and the refugees, were distributed (by Japanese soldiers).

Likewise health squads began to carry on medical and remedial work. Those who had serious eye diseases and had fallen into a condition approaching blindness were completely cured by the Japanese doctors. Children with whooping cough were carried in by their mothers for medical attention, and old women with diseased feet and great swellings received treatment. As soon as they tasted the flavor of the medicine, as soon as they enjoyed the beautiful taste of food, the crowds of refugees, their countenances beaming with joy, could not cease their thanksgiving. After the medical inspection and healing was over, the vast herds gathered around the soldiers beneath the Rising Sun flag and the Red Cross flag, shouting "Banzai" in order to express their gratitude. Along the road opposite, where a merchant was busy preparing to open his shop, a *hsien ping* (gendarme) smiled and passed a little chat. From the Drum Tower beside the Japanese Embassy, there is an elevation for a view around. Near the Embassy is hoisted the American flag; to the north and west, the British flag; to the south, the French; to the east the red flag of the Soviets is reflected in the jade waters of the lotus lake. Amid them all, high on the iron tower above the Japanese Embassy, is the Rising Sun streaming forth straight and true in the breeze. Looking down, one sees a playground for Nanking Children, with soldiers and Chinese children happy together, playing joyfully on the slides. Nanking is now the best place for all countries to watch, for here one breathes the atmosphere of peaceful residence and happy work.

This book has been produced wholly under union conditions. The paper was made, the type set, the plates electrotyped, and the printing and binding done in union shops affiliated with the American Federation of Labor. All employees of Modern Age Books, Inc., are members of the Book and Magazine Guild, Local No. 18 of the United Office and Professional Workers of America, affiliated with the Committee for Industrial Organization.

Recent Modern Age Titles of Interest to Readers of This Book

(Unless Otherwise Indicated, Books Are 5½ by 7½ Inches in Size, Bound in Sturdy Card Covers. *Indicates Reprint.)

Number   Price

63 SCHOOL FOR BARBARIANS: Education Under the Nazis, by Erika Mann, with an introduction by her father, Thomas Mann.   **50¢**

    The ominous story of goose-stepping, straight-jacketed German youth.

69 ONE-FIFTH OF MANKIND: China Fights For Freedom, by Anna Louise Strong.   **50¢**

    From her intimate first-hand experience the author of "I Change Worlds" untangles and interprets the fateful events in the Far East.

65 SAFE CONDUCT: Or When to Behave and Why, by Margaret Fishback, with illustrations by Helen E. Hokinson. Size 5½ x 8 inches.   **75¢**

    The irrepressible author of "Out of My Head" spoofs etiquette, but manages to convey much good sense in the process.

At Your Book Store
Or Write to

MODERN AGE BOOKS, INC.
432 Fourth Avenue   •   New York City

Number		Price
60	THE RIGHT TO WORK, by Nels Anderson.	**50¢**

The Labor Relations Director of the W.P.A. explains the vast benefits of public works.

59 LABOR'S NEW MILLIONS, by Mary Heaton Vorse. **50¢**

A veteran labor reporter brilliantly interprets the great recent organizational upsurge in America.

43 *THE PASTURES OF HEAVEN, by John Steinbeck. **25¢**

This early novel by the author of *Tortilla Flat* and *Of Mice and Men* is considered by many to be his best. It has the same enchantment and tenderness as the later books.

48 YOU CAN'T DO THAT, by George Seldes. **50¢**

A searching study of the sinister forces in America which, under the guise of patriotism, make a mockery of the civil liberties for which we have fought so bitterly.

42 *FONTAMARA, by Ignazio Silone. **35¢**

A great novel about Fascist Italy—a nearly incredible but true story of a lost cause in a small Italian village.

41 *CITIES OF SIN, by Hendrik de Leeuw. **35¢**

The story of prostitution and the white slave traffic in six great cities of the Orient—Yokohama, Hong Kong, Shanghai, Macao, Port Said, and Singapore.

39 LOVE, HERE IS MY HAT, by William Saroyan. **25¢**

Sixteen new and provocative stories by the author of *The Daring Young Man on the Flying Trapeze* (Modern Age Reprint No. 17 —25c).

At Your Book Store

Or Write to

MODERN AGE BOOKS, INC.

432 Fourth Avenue • New York City

CPSIA information can be obtained
at www.ICGtesting.com
Printed in the USA
LVHW082145120322
713324LV00007B/233